how work
for
GOD

ANDREW MURRAY

Formerly entitled WORKING FOR GOD

Whitaker House
PITTSBURGH & COLFAX STREETS, SPRINGDALE, PA. 15144

HOW TO WORK FOR GOD

ISBN: 0-88368-129-3
Printed in the United States of America
Copyright © 1983 by Whitaker House

Whitaker House
580 Pittsburgh Street
Springdale, PA 15144

4 5 6 7 8 9 10 11 12 13 / 05 04 03 02 01 00 99 98 97 96 95

CONTENTS

INTRODUCTION

The object of this book is first of all to remind all Christians of the greatness and the glory of the work in which God gives each of us a share. It is nothing less than the work of bringing men back to God, in which God finds His highest glory and blessedness. As we see that it is God's own work we have to perform, that He works it through us, that in our doing it His glory rests on us and we glorify Him, we will count it our joy to give ourselves to live completely for it.

At the same time, the aim of the book is to help those who complain that they are apparently laboring in vain—to find out what causes so much failure. God's work must be done in God's way and in God's power. It is spiritual work to be done by spiritual men in the power of the Spirit. Our joy in God's work will be greater the more we understand and submit ourselves to His laws of work.

Along with this I have in mind the great number of Christians who take little real part in the service of their Lord. They have never understood that the chief characteristic of the divine life in God and Christ is love and its work of blessing men. The divine life in us can show itself in no other way. I have tried to show that it is God's will that every believer without exception, whatever his position in life, gives himself totally to live and work for God.

I have also written in the hope that some, who train others in Christian life and work, may find thoughts presented here to be of use to them in teaching the imperative duty, the urgent need, the divine blessedness of a life given to God's service. May these teachers also learn to awaken within the consciousness of the power that works in them, even the Spirit and power of Christ Himself.

To the great host of workers in all the various forms of the ministry of love throughout the world, I lovingly offer these meditations, with the fervent prayer that God, the Great Worker, may make us true fellow-workers with Himself.

Andrew Murray

Chapter 1

Waiting And Working

"But they that wait upon the Lord shall renew their strength"—Isaiah 40:31.

"Neither hath the eye seen, O God, beside Thee, what He hath prepared for him that waiteth for Him"—Isaiah 64:4.

The relationship between waiting and working is made clear in the above verses. We see that waiting brings the needed strength for working—preparing us for joyful and unwearied work. "They that wait on the Lord shall renew their strength; they shall mount up with wings as eagles; they shall run, and not be weary; they shall walk, and not faint." Waiting on God has its value in this: it makes us strong to do His work. The second verse reveals the secret of this strength. "Neither hath the eye seen. . .what He hath prepared for him that waiteth for Him." The waiting on God secures the working of God for us and in us, out of which our work must spring. The two passages teach the great lesson that waiting on God lies at the root of all true working for God.

Our great need is to hold the two sides of this truth in perfect harmony.

There are some who say they wait upon God, but they do not work for Him. There may be various reasons for this. They confuse true waiting on God (living in direct communication with Him) with the lazy, helpless waiting that excuses itself from all work. Some wait on God as one of the highest exercises of the Christian life. Yet, they have never understood that the root of all true waiting must be surrender and readiness to be completely equipped for God's use in serving men. Others are ready to work as well as wait, but are looking for some great inflow of the Spirit's power to enable them to do mighty works, while they forget that as believers they already have the Spirit of Christ dwelling in them. They forget that more grace is only given to those who are faithful in the little, and that it is only in working that we can be taught by the Spirit how to do the greater works.

All Christians need to learn that waiting has working for its object. It is only in working that waiting can attain its full perfection and blessedness. It is as we elevate working for God to its true place, as the highest exercise of spiritual privilege and power, that the absolute need and the divine blessing of waiting on God can be fully known.

On the other hand, there are many who work for God but know little of what it is to wait on Him. They have been led to take up Christian work under the impulse of natural or spiritual feeling or

8

the urging of a pastor. However, they do so with very little sense of what a holy thing it is to work for God. They do not know that *God's work can only be done in God's strength, by God Himself working in us.*

The Son of God could do nothing of Himself. The Father in Him did the work as He lived in continual dependence before Him. Many have never learned that the believer can do nothing unless God works in him. They do not understand it is only in utter weakness we depend upon Him so His power can rest on us. They have no conception of a continual waiting on God as being one of the first and essential conditions of successful work. Christ's Church and the world are sufferers today, not only because so many of its members are not working for God, but because so much working for God is done without waiting on God.

Among the members of the body of Christ there is a great diversity of gifts and operations. Some who are confined to their homes because of sickness or other duties may have more time for waiting on God. Others, who are overworked, find it very difficult to make time and be quiet before the Lord. These may mutually supply each other's lack.

Let those who have time for waiting on God definitely link themselves to some who are working. Let those who are working seek the help of those to whom the special ministry of waiting on God has been entrusted. Thus will the unity and the health of the Church be maintained. Those who wait will know that the outcome will be power for work. Those who work will realize their only strength is the grace obtained by waiting. Thus will God work for His Church that waits on Him.

Let us pray as we proceed in these meditations on working for God that the Holy Spirit will show us how sacred and urgent our calling is to work, and how absolute our dependence is upon God's strength to work in us. May we also learn how sure it is that those who wait on Him will renew their strength. Then we will find waiting on God and working for God to be inseparably one.

1. It is only as God works for me, and in me, that I can work for Him.

2. All His work for me is through His life in me.

3. He will most surely work, if I wait on Him.

4. All His working for me, and my waiting on Him, has but one aim, to fit me for His work of saving men.

Chapter 2

Good Works The Light Of The World

"Ye are the light of the world. . . . Let your light shine so before men, that they may see your good works, and glorify your Father which is in heaven"—Matthew 5:14,16.

A light is meant for those in darkness to see. The sun lights up the darkness of this world. A lamp is hung in a room to give it light. The Church of Christ is the light of men. The god of this world has blinded their eyes. Christ's disciples are to shine into the darkness and give light. Just as the rays of light stream forth from the sun and scatter that light all about, the light of the good works of believers streams out to conquer the surrounding darkness with its ignorance of God and alienation from Him.

What a high and holy place is thus given to our good works! What power is attributed to them! How much depends upon them! They are not only the light and health and joy of our own lives, but the means of bringing lost souls out of darkness into God's marvelous light. They not only bless men, they glorify God in leading men to know Him as the Author of the grace seen in His children. Study the teaching of Scripture in regard to good works, especially all work done directly for God and His Kingdom. Let us listen to what these words of the Master have to teach us.

The aim of good works is that God may be glorified. You remember how our Lord said to the Father: "I have glorified Thee on the earth: I have finished the work which Thou gavest Me to do" (John 17:4). More than once we read of how the people glorified God because of His miracles. It was because what He had done was manifested by a divine power. Thus it is when our good works are something more than the ordinary virtues of refined men, and bear the imprint of God upon them, that men will glorify God. They must be the good works of which the Sermon on the Mount is the embodiment—a life of God's children, doing more than others, seeking to be perfect as their Father in heaven is perfect. When Christians glorify God and reflect His love, they help prepare the unsaved for conversion. The works prepare the way for the testimony and demonstrate the reality of the divine truth that is taught.

The whole world was made for the glory of God. Christ came to redeem us from sin and bring us back to serve and glorify Him. Believers are placed in the world with this one object, that they may let their light shine in good works, so as to win men to God. As truly as the light of the sun is meant to light up the world, the good works of God's children are meant to be the light of those who do not know or love God. We must clearly understand that good works bear the mark of something heavenly and divine and have the power of God in them.

The power is in good works. Of Christ it is written: "In Him was life; and the life was the light of men" (John 1:4). The divine life gave out a divine light. Of His disciples Christ said: "He that followeth Me shall not walk in darkness, but shall have the light of life" (John 8:12). Christ is our life and light. The deepest meaning of "Let your light shine" is, let Christ, who dwells in you, be seen by all you meet. And because Christ in you is your light, your humble works can carry with them a power of divine conviction. The divine power working in you will be the same power working in those who see your works. Give way to the Life and Light of Christ dwelling in you, and men will glorify your Father which is in heaven for what they see in your good works.

There is an urgent need of good works in believers. As it is necessary that the sun shines every day, it is even more necessary that every believer lets his light shine before men. We have been created anew in Christ for this—to hold forth the Word of Life as lights in the world. Christ needs you urgently to let His light shine through you. The unsaved around you need your light if they are to find their way to God. God needs you to let His glory be seen through you. Just as a lamp functions to light up a room, every believer should function to light up the world.

Let us study what working for God is, and what good works are as part of this. We will then desire to follow Christ fully and have the light of life shine into our hearts and lives and, from us, to the world.

1. *"Ye are the light of the world!"* The words express the calling of the Church as a whole. The fulfillment of her duty will depend upon the faithfulness with which each individual member loves and lives for those around him.

2. In all our efforts to awaken the Church to evangelize the world, our first aim must be to raise the standard of life for the individual believer concerning the teaching: As truly as a candle only exists with the object of giving light in the darkness, *the one object of your existence is to be a light to men.*

3. Pray that God by His Holy Spirit will reveal to you that you have nothing to live for but to let the light and love of God shine upon souls.

Chapter 3

Son, Go Work

"Son, go work to-day in my vineyard"—Matthew 21:28.

The father had two sons. To each he gave the command to go and work in his vineyard. The one went, the other did not. God has given the command and the power to every child of His to work in His vineyard, with the world as the field. The majority of God's children are not working for Him, and the world is perishing.

Of all the mysteries that surround us in the world, one of the strangest and most incomprehensible is—that after hundreds of years the very name of Jesus should be unknown to so many.

Consider what this means. To restore the ruin sin had caused, God, the Almighty Creator, actually sent His own Son to the world to tell men of His love and to bring them His life and salvation. When Christ made His disciples partakers of that salvation, and the unspeakable joy it brings, He emphasized that they should make it known to others and be the lights of the world. He spoke of

15

all who would come to Him through their witness. He left the world with the specific instruction to carry the Gospel to all men and teach all nations to practice all that He had commanded. He also gave the definite assurance that all power for this work was in Him. By the power of His Holy Spirit, He would enable His people to be witness to the ends of the earth. And what do we see now? Many have yet to hear the name of Jesus, and many act as though they never heard of Him!

Consider again what this means. All these dying millions have a right to come to the knowledge of Christ. Their salvation depends on their knowing Him. He could change their lives from sin and unhappiness to holy obedience and heavenly joy. Christ has a right to them. It would make His heart glad to have them come and be blessed in Him. Service to God is the connecting link. And yet, what His people do is nothing compared to what needs to be done, to what could be done, to what ought to be done.

What a revelation of the state of the Church! The great majority of those who are counted as believers are doing nothing toward making Christ known to their fellow-men. There are those who are entirely in Christ's service, but they are not free to conquer the world because they are occupied with teaching and helping weak Christians! And so, with a finished salvation, a loving Redeemer, and a Church set apart to spread the gospel, many are still perishing!

There can be nothing of greater importance to

the Church than to consider what can be done to awaken believers to a sense of their holy calling and to make them see that *to work for God,* they must offer themselves as instruments *through whom God can do His work.* The complaints that are continually heard of are a lack of enthusiasm for God's Kingdom in the majority of Christians and the vain attempts to awaken an interest in missions. Nothing less is needed than a revival that would raise the average Christian to an entirely new type of devotion. No true change can come until the truth is preached and accepted. The law of the Kingdom is: *Every believer is to live wholly for God's service and work.*

The father who called his sons to go work in his vineyard did not leave it to their choice to do as much or as little as they chose. They lived in his home. They were his children. He counted on what they would give him—their time and strength. God expects this of His children. Until it is understood that each child of God is to give His whole heart to his Father's interest and work as a worker for God, the evangelization of the world cannot be accomplished. Listen carefully and the Father will say to you, "Go work to-day in My vineyard."

1. Why is it that stirring appeals on behalf of missions often have so little permanent result? Because the command is brought to men who have not learned that absolute devotion and immediate obedience to the Lord is the essence of true salvation.

2. Once seen and confessed that the lack of interest in missions is the sign of a low and sickly Christian life, missions to every believer will make it their first aim to live completely for God. Every missionary meeting will be a consecration meeting to seek and surrender to the Holy Spirit's power.

3. The average standard of holiness and devotion cannot be higher at home or in the Church than in individual believers.

4. Everyone cannot go abroad, or give his whole time to direct work; but everyone, whatever his calling or circumstances, can give his whole heart to live for the winning of souls and the spreading of the Kingdom.

Chapter 4

To Each One His Work

"For the Son of man is as a man taking a far journey, who left his house, and gave authority to his servants, and to every man his work, and commanded the porter to watch"—Mark 13:34.

What I said about the failure of the Church to do the Master's work has often led me to ask: "What must be done to arouse the Church to a right sense of her calling?" This book attempts to give the answer. Working for God must take a very different and much more definite place in our teaching and training of Christ's disciples than it has done.

In studying the question, I have been very much helped by the life and writings of a great educator. The opening sentence of the preface to his biography states: "Edward Thring was unquestionably the most original and striking figure in the school-master world of his time in England." Thring attributes his own power and success to the prominence he gave to a few simple principles, and the faithfulness with which he carried them out at any sacrifice. I have found them helpful regarding the work of preaching as well as teaching, and to present them will help to clarify some of the chief lessons this book is meant to teach.

The basic principle that distinguished his teaching from what was current at the time was this: Every boy in school, regardless of ability, must have the same attention. At Eton, where he was educated and was first in his class, he saw the evil of the opposite system. Leaving the majority neglected, the school kept its prestige by training a number of men for the highest awards. He maintained that this was dishonest. There could be no truth in a school which did not care for all alike. Every boy had some gift. Every boy needed special attention. Every boy could, with care and patience, be fitted to know and fulfill his mission in life.

Apply this to the Church. Every believer has the calling to live and work for the Kingdom of his Lord. Every believer has an equal claim on the grace and power of the Holy Spirit, according to his gifts, to equip him for his work. And every believer has a right to be taught and helped by the Church for the service our Lord expects of him. When *every believer, even the weakest, is trained as a worker for God*, the Church can fulfill its mission. No one can be left out, because the Master gave His work to every one.

Another of Thring's principles was this: It is a law of nature that work is pleasure. Make it voluntary and not compulsory. Do not lead people blindly. Show them why they have to work, what its value will be, what interest can be awakened in it, what pleasure may be found in it.

What a field is opened for the preacher of the gospel taking charge of Christ's disciples. The preacher must clarify the greatness, the glory, the divine blessedness of the work to be done. The preacher must show the value in the carrying out of God's will and gaining His approval. The preacher must lead us in becoming the benefactors and saviors of the unsaved. The preacher must lead us in developing that spiritual vigor, that nobility of character, that spirit of self-sacrifice which leads to the true bearing of Christ's image.

A third truth on which Thring particularly insisted was the need of inspiring the belief in the assurance of attaining the goal. That goal is not to gain extensive knowledge, but rather, to cultivate the power to learn—this alone is true education. As a learner's powers of observation grow under guidance and teaching, he finds within himself a source of power and pleasure he never knew before. He feels a new self beginning to live, and the world around him gets a new meaning. "He becomes conscious of an infinity of unsuspected glory in the midst of which we go about our daily tasks, and becomes lord of an endless kingdom full of light and pleasure and power."

If this is the law and blessing of a true education, what light is shed on the calling of all teachers and leaders in Christ's Church! The *know ye nots* of Scripture—that ye are the temple of God—that Christ is in you—that the Holy Spirit dwells in you—acquire a new meaning. It tells us that the one thing that needs to be awakened in the hearts of Christians is the faith in "the power that worketh in us" (Ephesians 3:20). As one comes to see the worth and the glory of the work to be done—as one believes in the possibility of his, too, being able to do that work well—as one learns to trust the very power and very Spirit of God working in him "he will, in the fullest sense, become conscious of a new life, with an infinity of unsuspected glory in the midst of which we go about our daily task, and become lord of an endless kingdom full of light and pleasure and power." This is the royal life to which God has called all His people. The true Christian is one who knows God's power working in himself, and finds it his true joy to have the very life of God flowing into him, through him, and out from him to those around.

1. We must learn to believe in the value of every individual believer. As men are saved one by one, they must be trained one by one for work.

2. We must believe that work for Christ can become as natural, as much an attraction and a pleasure in the spiritual, as in the natural world.

3. We must believe and teach that every believer can become an effective worker in his area of work. Are you seeking to be filled with love for souls?

Chapter 5

To Each According To His Ability

"For the kingdom of heaven is as a man travelling into a far country, who called his own servants, and delivered unto them his goods. And unto one he gave five talents, to another two, to another one; to every man according to his several ability; and straightway took his journey"—Matthew 25:14-15.

In the parable of the talents, we have an instructive summary of our Lord's teaching in regard to the work He has given to His servants to do. He tells us He is going to heaven and leaving His work on earth to the care of His Church. He tells us He is giving every one something to do, however different the gifts might be. He tells us He is expecting to get back His money with interest. He tells us of the failure of him who received least and what it was that led to that terrible neglect.

"He called his own servants, and delivered unto them his goods. . .and straightway took his journey." This is literally what our Lord did. He went to heaven, leaving His work with all His

23

goods to the care of His Church. His goods were the riches of His grace, spiritual blessings in heavenly places, and His Word and Spirit. He gave in these to His servants to be used in carrying out His work on earth. They were to continue the work he had begun. Our Lord took His people into partnership with Himself, and entrusted His work on earth entirely to their care. Their neglect would cause it to suffer. Their diligence would be His enrichment. Here we have the true basic principle of Christian service—Christ has made Himself dependent on the faithfulness of His people for the extension of His Kingdom.

"Unto one he gave five talents, to another two, to another one; to every man according to his several ability." Though there was a difference in the measure, everyone received a portion of the master's goods. It is in connection with the service we are to provide each other that we read, "unto every one of us is given grace according to the measure of the gift of Christ" (Ephesians 4:7). This truth, that *every believer without exception has been set apart to take an active part in the work of winning the world for Christ,* has almost been lost. Christ was first a son, then a servant. Every believer is first a child of God, then a servant. It is the highest honor of a son to be a servant, to have the father's work entrusted to him. Neither the home nor the foreign missionary work of the Church will ever be done right until *every believer feels that the one object of his being in the world* is to work for the Kingdom. The first

duty of the servants in the parable was to spend their lives in caring for their master's interests.

"After a long time the lord of those servants cometh, and reckoneth with them" (Matthew 25:19). Christ keeps watch over the work He has left to be done on earth. His Kingdom and glory depend upon it. He will not only hold us accountable when He comes again to judge, but comes unceasingly to ask His servants about their welfare and work. He comes to approve and encourage, to correct and warn. By his Word and Spirit, He questions whether we are using our talents diligently and, as His devoted servants, questions whether we are living only and entirely for His work. He finds some laboring diligently, and to them He frequently says: "Enter thou into the joy of thy Lord" (Matthew 25:21). He sees that others are discouraged, and He inspires them with new hope. He finds some working in their own strength. These He reprimands. Still others He finds sleeping or hiding their talents. To such His voice speaks in solemn warning: "From him that hath not shall be taken away even that which he hath" Christ's heart is in His work (Matthew 25:29). Every day He watches over it with the keenest interest. Let us not disappoint Him nor deceive ourselves.

"I was afraid, and went and hid thy talent in the earth"(Matthew 25:25). It is a deeply solemn lesson that the man of the one talent was the one to fail and be so severely punished. It calls the Church to beware. By neglecting to teach the

25

weaker ones that their service is needed also, she lets their gifts lie unused. In teaching the great truth that every branch is to bear fruit, the Church must lay special emphasis on the danger of thinking this is only expected of the strong and advanced Christian. When Truth reigns in a school, the most backward pupils receive the same attention as the more clever pupils. Care must be taken that the weakest Christians receive special training, so that they, too, may joyfully have their share in the service of their Lord and all the blessedness it brings. If Christ's work is to be done, not one can be missed.

"Lord, I knew thee that thou art an hard man. . . .and I was afraid"(Matthew 25:24,25). Failure in service is caused chiefly by wrong thoughts of God and looking upon His service as that of a hard master. If the Church is to care for the weak ones who are apt to be discouraged, we must teach them what God says of the sufficiency of grace and the certainty of success. They must learn to believe that *the power of the Holy Spirit within them fits them for the work to which God has called them*. They must learn to understand that God Himself will strengthen the inner man with might by His Spirit. They must be taught that work is joy, health and strength. Unbelief lies at the root of laziness. Faith opens the eyes to see the blessedness of God's service, the sufficiency of His strength, and His rich rewards. The Church must awake to her calling to train the weakest of her members to know that Christ counts upon every

redeemed individual to live entirely for His work. This alone is true Christianity. This alone is full salvation.

Chapter 6

Life And Work

"My meat is to do the will of Him that sent Me, and to finish His work"—John 4:34.

"I must work the works of Him that sent Me"—John 9:4.

"I have glorified Thee on the earth: I have finished the work which thou gavest Me to do. And now, O Father, glorify Thou Me with Thine own self"—John 17:4-5.

Carefully read again the words of our Lord at the beginning of the chapter, and see what divine glory there is in His work. In His work, Christ showed His own glory and the Father's glory. It was because of the work He had done, and because He had glorified the Father in it, that He claimed to share the glory of the Father in heaven. He performed the great works so that the Father might be glorified. Work is indeed the highest form of existence, the highest manifestation of the divine glory in the Father and in His Son.

What is true of God is true of men. Life is action and reveals itself in what it accomplishes. The bodily life, the intellectual, the moral, the spiritual life—individual, social, national life—each of these is judged by its work. The character and quality of the work depends on the life—as the life, so the work. And, on the other hand, the life *depends* on the work. Without this there can be no full development and manifestation and perfecting of the life—as the work, so the life.

This is especially true of the spiritual life—the life of the Spirit in us. There may be a great deal of religious work which is the result of human will and effort. But there is little true worth and power, because the divine life is weak. When the believer does not know that Christ is living in him and does not know the Spirit and power of God working in him, there may be much sincerity and diligence, with little that lasts for eternity. On the contrary, there may be much external weakness and apparent failure, and yet results prove that the life is indeed of God.

The work depends upon the life. And the life depends on the work for its growth and perfection. All life has a destiny. It cannot accomplish its purpose without work. Life is perfected by work. The highest manifestation of its hidden nature and power comes out in its work. And so work is the great factor by which the hidden beauty and the divine possibilities of the Christian life are revealed. Work must not only be performed by the child of God for the result of being used as God's instrument, it must be given the same place it has in God Himself. As in the Father and the Son, and with the Holy Spirit dwelling in us, work is the highest manifestation of life.

Work must be restored to its right place in God's scheme of the Christian life as the highest form of existence. As God never ceases to perform His work of love and blessing in us and through us, so our performing what He works in us is our highest proof of being created anew in His likeness.

Working for God must have much greater prominence given to it if God's purposes are to be carried out. Every believer must be taught that work is to be our highest glory as it is the only perfect manifestation and, therefore, the perfection of life in God throughout the world. We must ask if it is to be so in our own lives.

If our work is to be our highest glory we must remember two things: *It can only come by beginning to work*. Those who have not had their attention directed to it cannot realize how great the temptation is to make work a matter of thought, prayer and purpose, without its really being *done*. It is easier to hear than to think, easier to think than to speak, easier to speak than to act. We may listen and accept and admire God's will, and in our prayer profess our willingness to do, and yet not actually *do* it. Let us take up our calling as God's working men, and do work hard for Him. Doing is the best teacher. If you want to know how to do a thing, begin and do it.

Then you will be able to understand the second aspect: *There is sufficient grace in Christ for all the work you have to do*. You will see with ever-increasing gladness how He, the Head, works all in you, the member. You will see how work for God may become your closest and fullest fellowship with Christ—your highest participation in the power of His risen and glorified life.

1. Beware of separating life and work. The more work you have, the more your work appears a failure. The more unfit you feel for work, the more time and care you should take to have your inner life renewed in close fellowship with God.

2. Christ lives in me—is the secret of joy and hope, and also of power for work. Care for the life and the life will care for the work. "Be filled with the Holy Ghost" (Acts 9:17).

Chapter 7

The Father Abiding In Me Does The Work

"But Jesus answered them, My Father worketh hitherto, and I work"—John 5:17.

"Believest thou not that I am in the Father, and the Father in Me? the words that I speak unto you I speak not of Myself: but the Father that dwelleth in Me, He doeth the works"—John 14:10.

Jesus Christ became man that He might show us what a true man is. He became man to show us how God meant to live and work in man. And He became man to show us how we can find purpose in our lives and do our work in God. In words like those above, our Lord opens up the inner mystery of His life and reveals to us the nature and the deepest secret of His working. He did not come to the world to work instead of the Father. Christ's work was the fruit, the earthly reflection of the Father working. And it was not as if Christ merely saw and copied what the Father willed or did— "the Father *that dwelleth in Me,* He doeth the works." Christ did all His work in the power of the Father living and working in Him. So complete and real was His dependence on the Father, that, in explaining it to the Jews, He used the strong expressions in John 5:19,30: "The Son can do nothing of Himself, but what He seeth the Father do." "I can of Mine own self do nothing." What He said is as true of us, "for without Me ye can do nothing" (John 15:5), as is it is true of Him too. "The Father that dwelleth in Me, He doeth the works."

Jesus Christ became man that He might show us: what true man is, what the true relationship between man and God is, and what the true way of serving God and doing His work is. When we are made new creatures in Christ Jesus, the life we receive is the very life that was and is in Christ. It is only by studying His life on earth that we know how we are to live. "As the living Father hath sent Me, and I live by the Father: so he that eateth Me, even he shall live by Me" (John 6:57).

Christ did not consider it a humiliation to be able to do nothing of Himself—to be always and absolutely dependent on the Father. He counted it His highest glory because all His works were the works of the all-glorious God in Him. When will we understand that to wait on God, to bow before Him in perfect helplessness and let Him work everything in us, is our true nobility and the secret of the highest activity? This alone is the true Christ-life, the true life of every child of God. As this life is understood and maintained, the power for work will grow because the soul is in the attitude in which God can work in us, as the God who "is good unto them that wait for Him" (Lamentations 3:25).

It is in ignoring or neglecting the great truths that there can be no true work for God. The explanation of the extensive complaint of so much Christian activity with so little genuine result is *God works in us*, yes, but He cannot work fully in us *unless we live in absolute dependence on Him*. The revival which many are longing and praying for must begin with this: the return of Christian ministers and workers to their true place before God—in Christ. And, like Christ, completely depend and continually wait on God to work in us.

I invite all workers, young and old, successful or disappointed, full of hope or full of fear, to come and learn from our Lord Jesus the secret of true work for God. "My Father worketh hitherto, and I work" (John 5:17). "The Father that dwelleth in Me, He doeth the works" (John 14:10). Divine Fatherhood means that God *is* all, and *gives* all, and *works* all. Continually depend on the Father, and receive, moment by moment, all the strength needed for His Work. Try to grasp the great truth that because "it is the same God which worketh all in all" (1 Corinthians 12:6), your one need is, in deep humility and weakness, to wait for and to trust in His working. From this, learn that God can only work in us as He dwells in us. "The Father that dwelleth in Me, He doeth the works." Cultivate the holy sense of God's continual nearness and presence, of your being His temple, and of His dwelling in you. Offer yourself for Him to work in you all His good pleasure. You will find that work, instead of being a hindrance, can become your greatest incentive to a life of fellowship and child-like dependence.

At first it may appear as if the waiting for God to work will keep you back from your work. It may indeed—but only to bring the greater blessing, when you have learned the lesson of faith that believes on His working even when you do not feel it. You may have to do your work in weakness and fear and much trembling. You will know the merit of the power is of God and not of yourself. As you know yourself better and God better, you will be content that it should always be—His strength made perfect in our weakness.

1. "The Father that dwelleth in Me, He doeth the works." There is the same law for the Head and the member, for Christ and the believer. "It is the same God that worketh all in all."

2. The Father worked in the Son while He was on earth, and now works through Him in heaven. It is as *we believe in the Father's working in Christ* that we will do the greater works. See John 14:10-12.

3. The indwelling and abiding God works in us. Allow God to live in you, and He will establish your good work.

4. Pray much for grace to say, in the name of Jesus, "The Father that dwelleth in Me, He doeth the works."

Chapter 8

Greater Works

"Verily, verily, I say unto you, He that believeth on Me, the works that I do shall he do also; and greater works than these shall he do; because I go unto My Father. And whatsoever ye shall ask in My name, that will I do, that the Father may be glorified in the Son. If ye shall ask any thing in My name, I will do it"—John 14:12-14.

In John 14:10, "the Father that dwelleth in Me, He doeth the works," Christ reveals the secret of all divine service—man yielding himself for God to dwell and to work in him. The law of God working in man remains unchanged when Christ promises, "He that believeth on Me, the works that I do shall he do also." If Christ says "The Father that dwelleth in Me, He doeth the works," how much more must *we* say it? With Christ and with us, it is "the same God which worketh all in all" (1 Corinthians 12:6).

We are taught how this is to be in the words, "He that believeth on Me." That not only means that we must believe Christ for salvation, as a Savior from sin. There is much more. In John 14:10,11 Christ said, *"The Father that dwelleth in Me, He doeth the works. Believe Me that I am in the Father, and the Father in Me."* We need to believe in Christ as the One in and through whom the Father unceasingly works. To believe in Christ is to receive Him into the heart. When we see the Father's working jointly with Christ, we know that to believe in Christ, and receive Him into our hearts, is to receive the Father dwelling in Him and working through Him. The works His disciples are to do cannot possibly be done in any other way than His own are done.

This becomes still more clear from what our Lord adds: "And greater works than these shall he do also; because I go unto My Father." It is clear what the greater works are. Three thousand were baptized by the disciples at Pentecost, and multitudes were added to the Lord afterwards. Philip at Samaria, the men of Cyprus and Cyrene, Barnabas at Antioch, Paul in his travels—always many people added to the Lord. Countless servants down to our day, have in the ingathering of souls, done these greater works in, for, with, and through Christ.

When the Lord says, "Because I go unto My Father," He clearly reveals the reason why we are enabled to do these greater works. When He entered the glory of the Father, all power in heaven and on earth was given to Him as our Redeemer. The Father was to work through Him in a way more glorious than ever. He was then to work through His disciples. His own work on earth received power from the Father in heaven. So His people, in their weakness, would do works like His, and greater works in the same way, through power received from heaven. The law of the divine working is unchangeable—*God's work can only be done by God Himself.* It is as we see this in Christ, and receive Him in this way, as the One in and through whom God works all, and yield ourselves completely to the Father working in Him and in us, that we shall do greater works than He did.

The words that follow bring out still more strongly the great truths we have been learning, that it is our Lord Himself who will work all in us, even as the Father did in Him, and that our attitude is to be exactly what His was—one of entire receptivity and dependence. "Greater works than these shall he do also; because I go unto My Father. And *whatsoever ye shall ask in My name, that will I do."* Christ connects the greater works the believer is to do *with the promise that He will do whatever the believer asks.* Prayer in the name of Jesus will be the expression of depending and waiting on Him for His working. He gives the promise: "Whatsoever ye ask. . .I will do," in you and through you. And when He adds, "that the Father may be glorified in the Son," He reminds us how He had glorified the Father, by yielding to Him as Father, to perform all His work in Himself as Son. In heaven Christ would still glorify the

Father, by receiving the power from the Father, and working in His disciples what the Father would. The believer, as Christ Himself, can give the Father no higher glory than yielding to Him to work all.

The believer can glorify the Father in no other way than by an absolute and unceasing dependence on the Son, in whom the Father works, to communicate and work in us all the Father's work. "If ye shall ask any thing in My name, *I will do it,*" and so, "greater works than these shall he do."

Let every believer strive to learn the blessed lesson—"I am to do the works I have seen Christ doing. I may even do greater works as I yield myself to Christ exalted on the throne in awesome power. I may count on Him working in me according to that power. My one need is the spirit of dependence and waiting, and prayer and faith, that Christ abiding in me will do the works, even whatsoever I ask."

1. How was Christ able to work the works of God? By God abiding in Him! How can I do the works of Christ? By Christ abiding in me!

2. How can I do greater works than Christ? By believing not only in Christ, the Incarnate and Crucified, but Christ triumphant on the throne.

3. In work everything depends, O believer, on the life, the inner life, the divine life. Pray to realize that work is vain except as it is in the power of the Holy Spirit dwelling in you.

Chapter 9

Created In Christ Jesus For Good Works

"For by grace are ye saved through faith; and that not of yourselves: it is the gift of God: Not of works, lest any man should boast. For we are His workmanship, created in Christ Jesus unto good works, which God hath before ordained that we should walk in them"—Ephesians 2:8-10.

We have been saved, not *of* works, but *for* good works. The difference is so great! The understanding of that difference is essential to the health of the Christian life. We are not saved *of* works which we have done. Yet we are saved *for* good works—the fruit and outcome of salvation, part of God's work in us, the one thing for which we have been created anew. Though our works are worthless in achieving salvation, their worth is infinite for which God has created and prepared us. We must seek to hold these two truths in the fullness of their spiritual meaning. The deeper our conviction that we have been saved, not of works, but of grace, the stronger the proof that we have been saved for good works.

"Not of works. . .for we are His workmanship."
If works could have saved us, there was no need
for our redemption. Because our works were all
sinful and vain, God undertook to make us anew.
We are now His workmanship, and all the good
works we do are His workmanship, too. "His
workmanship, created in Jesus Christ." So complete had been the ruin of sin, that God had to do
the work of creation over again in Jesus Christ. In
Him, and particularly in His resurrection from the
dead, He created us anew, after His own image,
into the likeness of the life which Christ had lived.
In the power of that life and resurrection, we are
able, we are perfectly equipped, for doing good
works. The eye, because it was *created* for the
light, is most perfectly adapted for its work. The
vine-branch, because it was *created* to bear
grapes, does its work so naturally. We, who have
been *created* in Jesus Christ for good works, may
be assured that a divine capacity for good works is
the very law of our being. If we but know and
believe in this our destiny, if we but live our lives
in Jesus Christ, as we were newly created in Him,
we can and will be fruitful unto every good work.

"Created. . .unto good works, which God hath
before ordained that we should walk in them." We
have been prepared for the works, and the works
prepared for us. To understand this, think of how
God pre-appointed His servants of old—Moses
and Joshua, Samuel and David, Peter and Paul—
for the work He had for them, and pre-appointed

41

equally the works He would have them do. The Father has prepared works for the humblest of His children as much as for those who are counted chief. God has a life-plan for each of his children, with work distributed according to the power and grace provided for the work. And so, just as the teaching *salvation not of works* is clear, so is its blessed counterpart, *salvation for good works* because God created us for them, and even pre-pared them for us.

The Scripture, therefore, confirms the double lesson this book desires to bring you. *Good works are God's design in the new life He has given you and ought to be your aim.* As every human being was created for work and endowed with the neces-sary energy, man can only live a true and healthy life by working. Every believer, then, exists to do good works. In them his life will be perfected, his fellow-men will be blessed, and his Father in heaven will be glorified. We educate all our chil-dren with the thought that they must go out and work in the world. When will the Church learn that its great work is to train every believer to take his share in *God's* great work and to abound in the good works for which he was created? We must each seek to take in the deep spiritual truth of the message, *"created in Christ Jesus unto good works, which God hath before ordained,"* and joyfully take up the work awaiting us and do it eagerly.

Waiting on God is the one great thing needed on our part if we would do the good works God has prepared for us. We must take into our hearts the holy meaning of these words: *We are God's workmanship,* not by one act in the past, but in a continuous operation. We are created for good works, as the great means for glorifying God. The good works are prepared for each of us that we might walk in them. Surrender to and dependence upon God's working is our one need. We must consider how our new creation for good works will become the habit of our soul and is all *in Christ Jesus,* and abiding *in Him,* believing *on Him,* and looking *for His strength alone. Created for good works* will reveal to us at once the divine command and the sufficient power to live a life in good works.

Let us pray for the Holy Spirit to work the Word into the very depths of our consciousness: *Created in Christ Jesus for good works!* In the light of this revelation, we will learn what a glorious destiny, what an infinite obligation, what a perfect capacity is ours.

1. Our creation in Adam was for good works. It resulted in entire failure. Our new creation in Christ is for good works again. But with this difference: perfect provision has been made for securing them.

2. God has created us for good works—let us pray for the Holy Spirit to show us and impart to us all this means.

3. If life in fellowship with God is true, the power for the work will be perfected. As the life, so the work.

Chapter 10

Work, For It Is God Who Works In You

"Work out your own salvation with fear and trembling. For it is God which worketh in you both to will and to do of His good pleasure"— Philippians 2:12-13.

In the last chapter we saw what salvation is. It is our being God's workmanship, created in Jesus Christ for good works. It concludes with one of its most important points. There is a treasury of good works which God has prepared for us to do. In the light of this thought, we get the true and full meaning of the scripture heading for this chapter. To work out your own salvation, such as God meant it to be, is to walk in all the good works which God has prepared for you. Study to know exactly what the salvation is that God has prepared for you (all that He has meant and made possible for you to be), and work it out with fear and trembling. Let the greatness of this divine and most holy life hidden in Christ, your own weakness, and the terrible dangers and temptations confronting you, make you work in fear and trem-

44

bling.

And yet, that fear never needs to become unbelief, nor that trembling discouragement, *for*—it is God which works in you. Here is the secret of a power that is absolutely sufficient for everything we have to do, the perfect assurance that we can do all that God really means us to do. God works in us both to will and to work. First, *to will*—He gives the insight into what is to be done, the desire that makes the work pleasure, the firm purpose of the will that masters the whole being, and makes it ready and eager for action. And then, *to work*—He does not give us the will and then leave us unaided to work it out ourselves. The will may see and accept the work, and yet lack the power to perform it. In the seventh chapter of Romans, we see that the new man delights in God's law, and yet is ill-equipped *to do* because of the war between the flesh and the Spirit. However, by the law of the Spirit of life in Christ Jesus, man was set free from the law of sin and death. Thus, the righteousness of the law could be fulfilled in Him as one who did not walk after the flesh but after the Spirit.

One great reason why believers fail in their work is that they think since God has given them the will to do it, they will automatically work in the strength of that will. They have never learned the lesson that because God has created us in Christ Jesus for good works and has prepared the good works in which we are to walk, He must work them all in us Himself. They have never listened very long to the voice speaking, "it is God which worketh in you."

Here is one of the deepest, most spiritual, and most precious truths of Scripture—the unceasing operation of Almighty God in our hearts and lives. In light of the very nature of God, as a spiritual being not confined to any place, but present everywhere, there can be no spiritual life unless it is supported by His personal indwelling.

Scripture states the deepest reason—*He worketh all in all.* Not only *of* Him are all things as their first beginning, and *to* Him as their end, but also *through* Him, who alone *maintains* them.

The Father was the source of all Christ did. In the new man, created *in* Jesus Christ, the unceasing dependence on the Father is our highest privilege, our true nobility. This is indeed fellowship with God—God Himself working in us to will and to do.

We must seek to learn the true secret of working for God. It is not, as many think, that we do our best and then leave God to do the rest. By no means. Rather, it is this, that we know that God's working His salvation *in* us is the secret of our working it *out*—that salvation includes *every* work we have to do. *The faith of God working in us is the measure of our fitness to work effectively.* The promises, "According to your faith be it unto you" (Matthew 9:29) and "All things are possible to him that believeth" (Mark 9:23), have their full application here. *The deeper our faith in God's working in us, the more freely the power of God will work in us, and the more true and fruitful our work will be.*

Perhaps some Sunday school worker is reading this. Have you really believed that your only power to do God's work is as one who has been created in Jesus Christ for good works, as one in whom God Himself works to will and to work? Have you yielded yourself to wait for that working? Do you work because you know God works in you? Do not say that these thoughts are too high. The work of leading young souls to Christ is too high for us, but if we live as little children in believing that God will work all in us, we will do His work in His strength. Pray much to learn and practice the lesson in all you do. Work, for God works in you.

1. I think we begin to feel that the spiritual apprehension of this great truth, "God worketh in you," is what all workers greatly need.

2. The Holy Spirit is the mighty power of God, dwelling in believers for life and for work. Ask God to show you that in all our service our first care must be the daily renewing of the Holy Spirit.

3. Obey the command to be filled with the Holy Spirit. Believe in His indwelling. Wait for His teaching. Yield to His leading. Pray for His mighty working. Live in the Spirit.

4. What the mighty power of God works in us we are surely able to do. Only give way to the power working in you.

Chapter 11

Faith Working By Love

"For in Jesus Christ neither circumcisions availeth any thing, nor uncircumcision; but faith which worketh by love. . . .but by love serve one another. For all the law is fulfilled in one word, even in this; Thou shalt love thy neighbor as thyself"—Galatians 5:6,13,14.

In Jesus Christ no external privilege is an advantage. The Jew might boast of his circumcision, the token of God's covenant. The Gentile might boast of his uncircumcision, with an entrance into the Kingdom free from the Jewish laws. Neither was of use in the Kingdom of heaven—nothing but, as in Galatians 6:15, a new creature, in which old things are passed away and all things become new. Or, as our text describes it—nothing but *faith working by love,* causing us to serve one another in love.

What a perfect description of the new life. First you have faith, as the root, planted and rooted in Jesus Christ. Then, as its aim, you have works as the fruit. And then between the two, as the tree,

48

growing down into the root and bearing the fruit upward, you have love, with the life-sap flowing through it by which the root brings forth the fruit. We do not need to speak of faith here. We have seen how believing in Jesus does the greater works, and we have seen how faith in the new creation and in God working in us is the secret of all work. Nor do we need to speak here of works. The whole book aims at securing them in place in every heart and life just as they are in God's heart and in His Word.

We must especially study the great truth that all work is to be love. Faith cannot do its work except through love. No works can have any worth unless they come from love. Love alone is the sufficient strength for all the work we have to do.

The power for work is love. It was love that moved God to all His work in creation and redemption. It was love that enabled Christ as man to work and to suffer as He did. It is love that can inspire us with the power of a self-sacrifice that does not seek its own, but is ready to live and die for others. It is love that gives us the patience that refuses to give up on those who are unthankful or hardened. It is love that reaches and overcomes the most hopeless. Love is the power for work in ourselves and in those for whom we labor. Let us love as Christ loved us.

The power for love is faith. Faith roots its life in the life of Jesus Christ, which is all love. Faith knows, even when we cannot fully realize the wonderful gift that has been given into our hearts in the Holy Spirit's outpouring of God's love. A spring in the earth may often be hidden or stopped up. Until it is opened the fountain cannot flow out. Faith knows that there is a fountain of love within that can spring up into eternal life and can flow out as rivers of living waters. It assures us that we can love, that we have a divine power to love within us, as an inherent gift of our new nature.

The power to exercise and show love is work. There is no such thing as power apart from concrete realities. It only acts as it is exercised. Power at rest cannot be found or felt. This is particularly true of the Christian graces, hidden as they are amid the weakness of our human nature. It is only by *doing* that you know that you *have*. A grace must be performed before we can rejoice in its possession. This is the unspeakable blessedness of work, and makes it so essential to a healthy Christian life that it wakes up and strengthens love, and makes us partakers of its joy.

Faith working by love. In Jesus Christ nothing is of value but this. Workers for God! Believe this. Practice it. Thank God much for the fountain of eternal love opened within you. Pray fervently and frequently that God may strengthen you with might by the power of His Spirit in your inner man, so that, with Christ dwelling in you, you may be rooted and grounded in love. Live your daily life, then, in your own home, in all your dealings with men, in all your work, as a life of divine love. The ways of love are so gentle and heavenly, you may not learn them all at once. But be of good courage, only believe in the power that works in you, and yield yourself to the work of love. It will surely gain the victory.

Faith working by love. In Jesus Christ nothing is of value but this. Let me press home this message, too, on those who have never thought of working for God. Come and listen.

You owe everything to God's love. The salvation you have received is all love. God's one desire is *to fill you with His love* for His own satisfaction, for your own happiness, for the saving of men. Now, I ask you—will you not accept God's wonderful offer *to be filled with His love?* Oh! Come and give your heart and life to the joy and the service of His love. Believe that the fountain of love is within you. It will begin to flow as you make a channel for it by deeds of love. Whatever work for God you try to do, seek to put love into it. Pray for the spirit of love. Give yourself to live a life of love. Think how you can love those around you, by praying for them, by serving them, by laboring for their temporal and spiritual welfare. Faith working by love in Jesus Christ, this alone is of great value.

1. "And now abideth faith, hope, (love), these three; but the greatest of these is (love)" (1 Corinthians 13:13). There is no faith or hope in God. God is love. The most Godlike thing is love.

2. Love is the nature of God. When it is shed abroad in our hearts by the Holy Spirit, love becomes our new nature. Believe this, give yourself over to it and act it out.

3. Love is God's power to do His work. Love was Christ's power. To work for God pray earnestly to be filled with love for souls!

Chapter 12

Bearing Fruit In Every Good Work

"That ye might walk worthy of the Lord unto all pleasing, being fruitful in every good work, and increasing in the knowledge of God; Strengthened with all might, according to His glorious power, unto all patience and long-suffering with joyfulness"—Colossians 1:10-11.

There is a difference between fruit and work. Fruit is that which comes spontaneously, without thought or will, the natural and necessary outcome of a healthy life. Work, on the contrary, is the product of effort guided by intelligent thought and will. In the Chrisitian life we have the two elements in combination. All true work must be fruit, the growth and product of our inner life, the operation of God's Spirit within us. And yet all fruit must be work, the result of our deliberate purpose and effort. In the words, "being fruitful in every good work," we have the practical summing up of the truth taught in some previous chapters. Because God works by His life in us, the work we do is fruit. In having faith in His working, we desire to be used of Him and to bear fruit—work. The secret of all true work lies in the harmony between the perfect spontaneity that comes from God's life and Spirit animating us and our co-operation with Him as His intelligent fellow-laborers.

In the words "filled with the knowledge of His will in all wisdom and spiritual understanding" (Colossians 1:9), we have the human side, our need of knowledge and wisdom. In the words "Strengthened with all might, according to His glorious power," we have the divine side. God teaching and strengthening, and man learning to understand and patiently do His will. Such is the double life that will be fruitful in every good work.

It has been said of the Christian life that the natural man must first become spiritual, and then again the spiritual man must become natural. As the whole natural life becomes truly spiritual, all our work will partake of the nature of fruit, the outgrowth of the life of God within us. And as the spiritual again becomes perfectly natural to us, a second nature in which we are completely at home, all the fruit will bear the mark of true work, calling into full exercise every faculty of our being.

"*Being fruitful in every good work*" suggests again the great thought, that as an apple tree or a vine is planted solely for its fruit, so the great purpose of our redemption is that God may have us for His work and service. It has been well said—"the end of man is an *action* and not a thought, though it were of the noblest." It is in his work that the nobility of man's nature as ruler of the world is proved. It is for good works that we have been created anew in Christ Jesus. It is when men see our good works that our Father in heaven will be glorified and have the honor which is His due for His workmanship. In the parable of the vine, our Lord insisted on this. "He that abideth in Me and I in him, the same bringeth forth *much fruit*"(John 15:5). "Herein is My Father glorified, that ye bear *much fruit*" (John 15:8). Nothing gives more honor to a farmer than to succeed in raising an abundant crop—much fruit is glory to God.

The great need is that every believer be encouraged, helped, and even trained to aim at producing much fruit. A little strawberry plant may, in its measure, bear a more abundant crop than a large apple tree. The call to be fruitful in every good work is for every Christian without exception. The grace that is needed to do this is available to everyone. Every branch fruitful in every good work—this is an essential part of God's Gospel.

We must get a true impression of the two sides of the divine truth "being fruitful in every good work." God's first creation of life was in the vegetable kingdom. It was a life without anything of will or self-effort. All growth and fruit was simply His own direct work, the spontaneous outcome of His hidden working. There was progress in the creation of the animal kingdom. A new element was introduced—thought and will and work. In man these two elements were united in perfect harmony. The absolute dependence of the grass and the lily on the God who clothes them with their beauty was to be the groundwork of our relationship. Nature has nothing but what it receives from God. Our works are to be fruit, the product of a God-given power. But to this was added the true mark of our God-likeness, the power of will and independent action—all fruit is to be our own work. As we grasp this we will see how the most complete understanding of our having nothing in ourselves is consistent with the deepest sense of obligation and the strongest desire to exert our powers to the very utmost. We must study the lessons of the text as those who seek all their wisdom and strength from God alone. And we will boldly give ourselves, as those who are responsible for the use of that wisdom and strength, to the diligence, sacrifice and effort needed for a life bearing fruit in every good work.

1. Much depends, for quality and quantity, on the healthy life of the tree. The life of God, of Jesus Christ, of His Spirit—the divine life in you, must be strong and sure.

2. That life is love. Believe in it. Act it out. Have it replenished day by day out of the fullness there is in Christ.

3. Let all your work be fruit. Let all your willing and working be inspired by the life of God. So will you walk worthily of the Lord with all pleasing.

Chapter 13

Always Abounding In The Work Of The Lord

"Therefore, my beloved brethren, be ye sted-fast, unmoveable, always abounding in the work of the Lord, forasmuch as ye know that your labour is not in vain in the Lord"—1 Corinthians 15:58.

The fifteenth chapter of First Corinthians presents the divine revelation of the meaning of Christ's resurrection, with all its blessings.

It gives us a living Savior who revealed Himself to His disciples on earth and to Paul from heaven. It assures us of the complete deliverance from all sin. It is the pledge of His final victory over every enemy, when He gives up the Kingdom to the Father, and God is all in all. It assures us of the resurrection of the body and our entrance to heavenly life. Paul had closed his argument with his triumphant appeal to Death and Sin and the Law— "O death, where is thy sting? O grave where is thy victory?" (1 Corinthians 15:55). The sting of death is sin; and the strength of sin is the law. "But thanks be to God, which giveth us the victory through our Lord Jesus Christ" (1 Corinthians 15:57). And then, after fifty-seven verses of exultant teaching concerning the mystery and the glory of the resurrection life in our Lord and His people, there is one verse of practical application. "Therefore, my beloved brethren, be ye stedfast, unmoveable, always abounding in the work of the Lord." The faith in a risen, living Christ, and in all that His resurrection is to us in time and eternity, is to equip us for, is to prove itself in—abounding work for our Lord!

It cannot be otherwise. Christ's resurrection was His final victory over sin, death, and Satan. It was His entry to His work of giving the Spirit from heaven and extending His Kingdom throughout the earth. Those who shared the resurrection joy at once received the direction to make known the joyful news. It was so with Mary and the women. It was so with the disciples the evening of the resurrection day. "As My Father hath sent Me, even so send I you" (John 20:21). It was so with all to whom the charge was given—"Go ye into all the world, and preach the gospel to every creature" (Mark 16:15). The resurrection is the beginning and the pledge of Christ's victory over all the earth. That victory is to be carried out to its complete manifestation through His people. The faith and joy of the resurrection life are the inspiration and the power for the work of doing it. And so the call comes to all believers without exception— "Therefore, my beloved brethren, be ye. . .always abounding in the work of the Lord."

"In the work of the Lord." The connection tells us at once what that work is. It is nothing else or less than telling others of the risen Lord and proving to them what new life Christ has brought to us. As we indeed know and acknowledge Him as Lord over all we are, and live in the joy of His service, we will see that the work of the Lord is but one work—*that of winning men to know and bow to Him*. Amid all the forms of service, the one aim in the power of the life of the risen Lord is to make Him Lord of all.

This work of the Lord is no easy one. It cost Christ His life to conquer sin and Satan and gain the risen life. It will cost us our lives, too—the sacrifice of the life of nature. It needs the surrender of all on earth to live in the full power of resurrection newness of life. The power of sin and the world in those around us is strong. Satan does not easily give up his servants to our efforts. It needs a heart in close touch with the risen Lord, truly living the resurrection life, to be stedfast, unmoveable, *always abounding* in the work of the Lord. But that is a life that can be lived— because Jesus lives.

Paul adds: "Forasmuch as ye know that your labour is not in vain in the Lord" (1 Corinthians 15:58). I have spoken more than once of the mighty influence that the certainty of reward for work, in the shape of wages or riches, exerts on the millions of earth's workers. Christ's workers can, with assurance, believe that with such a Lord their reward is sure and great! The work is often difficult and slow, and apparently fruitless. We are apt to lose heart, because we are working in our strength and judging by our expectations. Listen to the message—"be ye. . .always abounding in the work of the Lord, forasmuch as ye know your labour is not in vain in the Lord." "Let not your hands be weak: for your work shall be rewarded" (2 Chronicles 15:7). "Ye know that your labour is not in vain in the Lord."

"In the Lord." The expression is a significant one. Study it in Romans 16, where it occurs ten times, where Paul uses the expressions: "Receive her in the Lord" (verse 2); "my helpers in Christ Jesus" (verse 3); "who also were in Christ before me" (verse 7); "beloved in the Lord" (verse 8); "approved in Christ" (verse 10); "who labour in the Lord" (verse 12); "chosen in the Lord" (verse 13). The entire life and fellowship and service of these saints had one mark—they were, their labors were, in the Lord. Here is the secret of effective service. "Your labour is not in vain *in the Lord.*" As a sense of His presence and the power of His life is maintained, as all works are produced in Him, His strength works in our weakness. Our labor cannot be in vain in the Lord. Christ said: "He that abideth *in Me,* and I in him, the same bringeth forth much fruit" (John 15:5). Do not let the children of this world, with their confidence that the masters whose work they are doing will certainly give them their due reward, put the children of light to shame. Let us rejoice and labor in the confident faith of the word: "Therefore,

beloved brethren, be ye. . .always abounding in
the work of the Lord. . .your labour is not in vain
in the Lord."

Chapter 14

Abounding Grace For Abounding Work

"And God is able to make all grace abound toward you; that ye, always having all sufficiency in all things, may abound to every good work"—2 Corinthians 9:8.

In the previous chapter we were motivated to abounding work—the spirit of triumphant joy which Christ's resurrection inspires as it covers the past and the future. This chapter assures us that for this abounding work we have the ability provided. God is able to make all grace abound, that we may abound to all good works. Every thought of abounding grace is to be connected with the abounding in good works for which it is given. And every thought of abounding work is to be connected with the abounding grace that equips us for it.

Abounding grace has *abounding work for its aim.* It is often thought that grace and good works are in disagreement with each other. This is not so. What Scripture calls the works of the law are our own works, the works of righteousness which we have done. They are dead works—works by which we seek to merit or to be made fit for God's favor. These are the very opposite of grace. But they are also the very opposite of the good works which spring *from* grace, for which grace is given. As incompatible as the works of the law are with the freedom of grace, the works of faith, good works, are essential and indispensable to the true Christian life. God makes grace abound, that good works may abound. The measure of true grace is tested and proved by the measure of good works. God's grace abounds in us that we may abound in good works. We need to have the truth deeply rooted in us. *Abounding grace has abounding work for its aim.*

Abounding work needs *abounding grace as its source and strength.* There often is abounding work without abounding grace. Just as any man may be very diligent in an earthly pursuit, or a heathen in his religious service of an idol, so men may be very diligent in doing religious work in their own strength, with but little thought of that grace which alone can do true, spiritual, effective work. For all work that is to be really acceptable to God, and truly fruitful, not only for some visible result here on earth, but for eternity, the grace of God is indispensable. Paul continually gives complete credit for his own work to the grace of God working in him. "I laboured more abundantly than they all: yet not I, but the grace of God which was with me" (1 Corinthians 15:10). "According to the gift of the grace of God given unto me by the effectual working of His power" (Ephesians 3:7). And he as frequently calls upon Christians to exercise their gifts "according to the grace that is given to us" (Romans 12:6). "But unto every one of us is given according to the measure of the gift of Christ" (Ephesians 4:7). It is only by the grace of God working in us that we can do what are truly good works. It is only as we seek and receive abounding grace that we can abound in every good work.

"God is able to make all grace abound toward you; that ye. . .may abound to every good work." Every Christian ought to praise God with great thanksgiving for the abounding grace that is thus provided for him. And with great humiliation confess that the experience of, and the surrender to, that abounding grace has been so defective. And with great confidence believe that a life abounding in good works is indeed possible, because the abounding grace for it is so sure and so divinely sufficient. And then, with great simple childlike dependence, wait upon God day by day to receive more grace which He gives to the humble.

Child of God! Take time to study and truly understand God's purpose with you, *that you abound in every good work!* He means it! He has provided for it! Make the measure of your consecration to Him nothing less than His purpose for you. And claim, then, nothing less than the abounding grace He is able to bestow. Make His omnipotence and His faithfulness your confidence. And live ever in the practice of continual prayer and dependence upon His power working in you. This will make you abound in every good work. "According to your faith be it unto you" (Matthew 9:29).

Christian worker, learn here the secret of all failure and all success. Work in our own strength, with little prayer and waiting on God for His Spirit, is the cause of failure. The cultivation of the spirit of absolute weakness and unceasing dependence will open the heart for the workings of the abounding grace. We will learn to credit all we do to God's grace. We will learn to measure all we have to do by God's grace. And our lives will increasingly be in the joy of God's making His grace abound in us, and our abounding in every good work.

1. "That ye may abound to every good work." Pray over this now until you feel that this is what God has prepared for you.

2. If your ignorance and weakness appear to make it impossible, present yourself to God and say you are willing, if He will enable you to abound in good works, to be a branch that brings forth much fruit.

3. Take into your heart, as a living seed, the precious truth: "He staggered not at the promise of God through unbelief; but was strong in faith, giving glory to God; And being fully persuaded that, what he had promised, he was able also to perform" (Romans 4:20,21). And "Faithful is He that calleth you, who will also do it" (1 Thessalonians 5:24).

4. Begin at once by doing lowly deeds of love. As the little child in kindergarten, *learn by doing*.

Chapter 15

In The Work Of Ministering

"And He gave some, apostles; and some, prophets; and some, evangelists; and some, pastors and teachers; For the perfecting of the saints, for the work of the ministry, for the edifying of the body of Christ"—Ephesians 4:11-12.

Christ's object, when He ascended to heaven and bestowed on His servants the various gifts that are mentioned, is threefold. Their first aim is—*for the perfecting of the saints.* Believers as saints are to be led on in the pursuit of holiness until they "stand perfect and complete in all the will of God" (Colossians 4:12). It was for this Epaphras labored in prayer. Paul writes of this: "Whom we preach. . .teaching every man in all wisdom; that we may present every man perfect in Christ Jesus" (Colossians 1:28).

This perfecting of the saints is, however, only a means to a higher end—*unto the work of ministering,* to equip all the saints to take part in the service to which every believer is called. The same word is used in texts such as: "which ministered unto Him of their substance" (Luke 8:3) and "ye have ministered to the saints, and do minister" (Hebrews 6:10). Two other examples of the use of this word are found in 1 Corinthians 16:15 and 1 Peter 4:11.

And this, again, is also a means to a still higher end—*unto the building up of the Body of Christ.* As every member of our body takes its part in working for the health and growth and maintenance of the whole, so every member of the Body of Christ is to consider it his first great duty to take part in all that can help to build up the Body of Christ. And this, whether by the helping and strengthening of those who are already members, or the ingathering of those who are to belong to it. And the great work of the Church is, through its pastors and teachers, to labor for *the perfecting of the saints* in holiness and love and fitness for service, that every one may take his part in *the work of ministering,* so that *the Body of Christ may be built up* and perfected.

Of the three great objects with which Christ has given His Church apostles and teachers, the work of ministering stands thus in the middle. On the one hand, it is preceded by that on which it absolutely depends—*the perfecting of the saints.* On the other hand, it is followed by that which it is meant to accomplish—*the building up of the Body of Christ.* Every believer without exception, every member of Christ's Body, is called to take part in the work of ministering. Every reader must try to realize the sacredness of his holy calling.

We must learn what the qualifications are for our work. "The perfecting of the saints" prepares them for the "work of ministering." It is the lack of true sainthood, of true holiness, that causes such scarce and weak service. As Christ's saints are taught and truly learn what conformity to Christ means, a life like His will become the one thing for which we live. His life was given up in self-sacrifice for the service and salvation of men. His humility and love, His separation from the world and devotion to the fallen, are seen to be the very essence and blessedness of the life He gives—the work of ministering, the ministry of love. Humility and love—these are the two great virtues of the saint—they are the two great powers for the work of ministering. Humility makes us willing to serve. Love makes us wise to know how to do it. Love is inventive. It seeks patiently, and suffers long, until it finds a way to reach its object. Humility and love are equally turned away from self and its claims. Let us pray, let the Church labor for "the perfecting of the saints" in humility and love, and the Holy Spirit will teach us how to minister.

We must look at what the great work is that the members of Christ have to do. It is to minister to each other. Place yourself at Christ's disposal for service to your fellow-Christians. Count yourself their servant. Study their interests. Set yourself actively to promote the welfare of the Christians around you. Selfishness may cause us to hesitate, the feeling of weakness may discourage us, laziness and comfort may raise difficulties for us. But, ask your Lord to reveal to you His will, and give yourself up to it. Round about you there are Christians who are cold and worldly and wandering from their Lord. Begin to think what you can do for them. Accept as the will of the Head that you as a member should care for them. Pray for the Spirit of love. Begin somewhere—only begin, and do not continue hearing and thinking while you do nothing. Begin the work of ministering "according to the measure of the gift of Christ" (Ephesians 4:7). He will give more grace.

We must believe in the power that works in us as sufficient for all we have to do. As I think of the thumb and finger holding the pen with which I write this, I ask, "How is it that during all these seventy years of my life they have always known just to do my will?" It was because the life of the head passed into and worked itself out in them. "He that believeth on Me," as his Head working in him, "the works that I do shall he do also." Faith in Christ, whose strength is made perfect in our weakness, will give the power for all we are called to do.

Let us cry to God that all believers may wake up to the power of this great truth—*Every member of the body is to live completely for the building up of the body.*

1. To be a true worker the first thing is close, humble fellowship with Christ the Head, to be guided and empowered by Him.

2. The next is humble, loving fellowship with Christ's members serving one another in love.

3. This prepares and equips us for service in the world.

Chapter 16

According To The Working
Of Each Several Part

*"May grow up into Him in all things, which is
the head, even Christ: From whom the whole
body fitly joined together and compacted by that
which every joint supplieth, according to the
effectual working in the measure of every part,
maketh increase of the body unto the edifying of
itself in love"*—Ephesians 4:15-16.

Paul is speaking here of the growth, the
increase, the building up of the body. This growth
and increase has, as we have seen, a double reference. It includes both the spiritual uniting and
strengthening of those who are already members
in order to secure the health of the whole body.
And also, to increase the body by the addition of
all who are as yet outside of it, and are to be
gathered into it. We spoke of the former in the
previous chapter—of the mutual interdependence
of all believers and the calling to care for each
other's welfare. In this chapter we look at the
growth from the other side—the calling of every

member of Christ's body to labor for its increase by the labor of love that seeks to bring in them who are not yet a part of it. This increase of the body and building up of itself in love can only be by the working in due measure of each several part.

Think of the body of a child. How does it reach the stature of a full-grown man? In no other way but by the working in due measure of every part. As each member takes its part, by the work it does in seeking and taking and assimilating food, the increase is made by its building up itself. The work that assures the growth comes from within, not without. In no other way can Christ's Body attain the stature of the fullness of Christ. As it is unto Christ the Head we grow up, and from Christ the Head the body increases itself, so it is through the contribution of every joint according to the working in due measure of each several part. Let us see what this implies.

The Body of Christ is to consist of all who believe in Him throughout the world. There is no possible way in which these members of the body can be gathered in, but by the body building itself up in love. Our Lord has made Himself, as Head, absolutely dependent on His members to do this work. What nature teaches us of our own bodies, Scripture teaches us of Christ's body. The head of a child may have thoughts and plans of growth— they will all be vain, except as the members all do their parts in securing that growth. Jesus Christ has committed to His Church the growth and increase of His Body. He asks and expects that as He the Head lives for the growth and welfare of the body, every member of His Body, the very weakest, must do the same, to build up the body in love. Every believer is to count it his one duty and blessedness to live and labor for the increase of the body, the ingathering of all who are to be its members.

What is it that is needed to bring the Church to accept this calling, and to train and help the members of the body to know and fulfill it? One thing. We must see that the new birth and faith and all insight into truth, with all resolve and surrender and effort to live according to it, is only a preparation for our true work. What is needed is that in every believer Jesus Christ be so formed, so dwell in the heart, that His life in us will be the impulse and inspiration of our love to the whole body and our life for it. It is because self occupies the heart that it is so easy and natural and pleasing to care for ourselves. When Jesus Christ lives in us, it will be as easy and natural and pleasing to live completely for the Body of Christ. As readily and naturally as the thumb and fingers respond to the will and movement of the head will the members of Christ's Body respond to the Head as the body grows up into Him, and from Him makes itself increase.

Let us sum this up. For the great work the Head is doing in gathering in from throughout the world and building up His Body, *He is entirely dependent on the service of the members*. Not only our Lord, but a perishing world is waiting and calling

for the Church to awake and give herself completely to this work—*the perfecting of the number of Christ's members*. Every believer, the very
weakest, must learn to know his calling—*to live
with this as the main purpose of this existence.*
This great truth will be revealed to us in power,
and obtain precedence as *we give ourselves to the
work of ministering* according to the grace *we
already have*. We may confidently wait *for the full
revelation of Christ in us as the power to do all
He asks of us.*

Chapter 17

Women Adorned With Good Work

"Women adorn themselves in modest apparel, with shamefacedness and sobriety; not with broided hair, or gold, or pearls, or costly array; But (which becometh women professing godliness) with good works"—1 Timothy 2:9-10.

"Let not a widow be taken into the number under threescore years old, having been the wife of one man, Well reported of for good works. . .if she have diligently followed every good work"—1 Timothy 5:9-10.

In the three Pastoral Epistles written to two young pastors to instruct them in regard to their duties, "good works" are more frequently mentioned than in Paul's other Epistles.[1] In writing to the churches, as in a chapter like Romans 12, he mentions the individual good work by name. In writing to the pastors he had to use this expression

---

[1]In 1 Timothy six times— 2:10; 3:1; 5:10; 5:25; 6:18. In 2 Timothy twice—2:21; 3:17. In Titus six times—1:16; 2:7,14; 3:1,8,14.

as a summary of their aim both in their own lives and their teaching of others. A minister was to be prepared and completely equipped to accomplish every good work—an example of good works. They were to teach Christians—the women to adorn themselves with good works, to follow diligently every good work, and to be well reported of for good works. The men were to be rich in good works, to be zealous of good works, to be ready for every good work, and to learn to maintain good works. No portion of God's work emphasizes more definitely the absolute necessity of good works as an essential, vital element in the Christian life.

Our two texts speak of the good works of Christian women. In the first they are taught that their adorning is to be not with fancy hair, and gold or pearls or costly clothing but, as becomes women preferring godliness, with good works. We know what adornment is. A leafless tree in winter has life. When spring comes it puts on its beautiful garments and rejoices in the adornment of foliage and blossom. The adorning of Christian women is not to be in hair or pearls or clothing, but in good works. Whether it is the good works that have reference to personal duty and conduct, or those works of charity that aim at the pleasing and helping of our neighbor, or those that more definitely seek the salvation of souls—the adorning that pleases God, that gives true heavenly beauty, that will truly attract others to come and serve God, too, is what Christian women ought to seek after. John saw the holy city descend from heaven, "prepared as a bride adorned for her husband": "The fine linen is the righteousness of saints" (Revelations 21:2; 19:8). If only every Christian woman might seek to adorn herself to please the Lord!

In the second passage we read of widows who were placed upon an honor roll in the early Church, and to whom a certain charge was given over the younger women. No one was to be enrolled who was not "well reported of for good works." Some of these are mentioned: if she has been known for the careful upbringing of her children, for her hospitality to strangers, for her washing the saint's feet, for her relieving the afflicted. And then there is added: "if she have *diligently followed every good work.*" If her life has been devoted to good works in her home and out of it, in caring for her own children, for strangers, for saints, she may indeed be counted fit to be an example and guide to others. The standard is a high one. It shows us the place good works took in the early Church. It shows how woman's blessed ministry of love was counted on and encouraged. It shows how, in the development of the Christian life, nothing so fits for rule and influence as a life given to good works.

Good works are part and parcel of the Christian life, equally indispensable to the health and growth of the individual, and to the welfare and extension of the Church. And yet, what multitudes of Christian women there are whose active share in the good work of blessing their fellow-creatures is little more than playing at good works. They are waiting for the preaching of a full gospel, which will encourage and help and compel them to give their lives to work so for their Lord, that they, too, may be well reported of as diligently following every good work.

The time and money, the thought and feeling given to jewels or costly clothing, will be exchanged for the true goal. Christianity will no longer be a selfish desire for personal safety, but the joy of being like Christ, the helper and savior of the needy. Work for Christ will take its true place as the highest form of existence, the true adornment of the Christian life. And as diligence in the pursuits of earth is honored as one of the true elements of character and worth, following good works diligently in Christ's service will be found to give access to the highest reward and the fullest joy of the Lord.

1. We are beginning to awaken to the wonderful place women can take in church and school mission. This truth needs to be brought home to every one of the King's daughters, that the adorning in which they are to attract the world, to please their Lord, and enter His presence is—good works.

2. Women, as "the meekness and gentleness of Christ" (2 Corinthians 10:1), are to teach man the beauty and the power of the long-suffering, self-sacrificing ministry of love.

3. The training for the service of love begins in the home life. It is strengthened in the inner chamber. It reaches out to the needy around, and finds its full scope in the world for which Christ

died.

Chapter 18

Rich In Good Works

"Charge them that are rich in this world. . . .That they do good, that they be rich in good works, ready to distribute, willing to communicate; Laying up in store for themselves a good foundation against the time to come, that they may lay hold on eternal life"—1 Timothy 6:17-19.

If women are to regard good works as their adornment, men are to count them their riches. As good works satisfy woman's eye and taste for beauty, they meet man's craving for possession and power. In the present world riches have a wonderful significance. They are often God's reward on diligence, industry, and enterprise. They represent and embody the life-power that has been spent in procuring them. As such, they exercise power in the honor or service they secure from others. Their danger consists in their being of this world, in their misdirecting the heart from the living God and heavenly treasures. They may become a man's deadliest enemy. How difficult it is for those who have riches to enter the kingdom of heaven!

The gospel never takes away anything from us without giving us something better in its place. It meets the desire for riches by the command to be rich in good works. The coin that is current in God's Kingdom is good works. The reward in the world to come will be determined according to these. By abounding in good works we lay up for ourselves treasures in heaven. Even here on earth they constitute a treasure, in the testimony of a good conscience, in the consciousness of being well-pleasing to God (1 John 3), in the power of blessing others.

There is more. Wealth of gold is not only a symbol of the heavenly riches. It is actually, though so opposite in its nature, a means to it. "Charge. . .the rich that they do good, that they be ready to distribute, willing to communicate; Laying up in store for themselves a good foundation." "Make to yourselves friends of the mammon of unrighteousness; that, when ye fail, they may receive you into everlasting habitations" (Luke 16:9). Even as the widow's mite, the gifts of the rich, when given in the same spirit, may be an offering with which God is well pleased (Hebrews 13:16).

The man who is rich in money may become rich in good works, if he follows the instructions in Scripture. The money must not be given to be seen of men, but as unto the Lord. Nor must it be given as from an owner, but a steward who administers the Lord's money with prayer for His guidance. Nor must it be given with any confidence in its power or influence, but in deep dependence on Him who alone can make it a blessing. Nor must it be given as a substitute for that personal work and witness which each believer is to give. As all Christian work, so our money-giving has its value alone from the spirit in which it is done, even the spirit of Christ Jesus.

What a field there is in the world for accumulating these riches, these heavenly treasures! In relieving the poor, in educating the neglected, in helping the lost, in bringing the gospel to Christians and heathens in darkness, what investment might be made if Christians sought to be rich in good works—rich toward God! We may well ask the question, "What can be done to awaken a desire for these true riches among believers?" Men have made a science of the wealth of nations and carefully studied all the laws by which its increase and universal distribution can be promoted. How can the order to be rich in good works convict hearts that its pursuit will be as much a pleasure and a passion as the desire for the riches of the present world?

All depends upon the nature, the spirit, of man. To the earthly nature, earthly riches have a natural affinity and irresistible attraction. To foster the desire for the acquisition of what constitutes wealth in the heavenly Kingdom, we must appeal to the spiritual nature. That spiritual nature needs to be taught and educated and trained into all the business habits that go into making a man rich.

There must be the ambition to rise above the level of a bare existence, the deadly contentment with just being saved. There must be some insight into the beauty and worth of good works as the expression of the divine life—God's working in us and our working in Him, as the means of bringing glory to God, as the source of life and blessing to men, as the laying up of a treasure in heaven for eternity. There must be a faith that these riches are actually within our reach, because the grace and Spirit of God are working in us. And there must be an outlook of doing the work of God to those around us at every opportunity, in the footsteps of Him who said, "It is more blessed to give than to receive" (Acts 20:35). Study and apply these principles. They will open the sure road to your becoming a rich man. A man who wants to be rich often begins on a small scale, but never loses an opportunity. Begin at once with some work of love, and ask *Christ, who became poor, that you might be rich,* to help you.

1. What is the cause that the appeal for money for missions meets with such insufficient response? It is because of the low spiritual state of the Church. Christians have no due conception of their calling to live completely for God and His Kingdom.

2. How can the evil be remedied? Only when believers see and accept their divine calling to make God's Kingdom their first care, and with humble confession of their sins yield themselves

to God, will they truly seek the heavenly riches to be found in working for God.

3. Never cease to plead and labor for a true spiritual awakening throughout the Church.

Chapter 19

Prepared Unto Every Good Work

"If a man therefore purge himself from these,
he shall be a vessel unto honour, sanctified, and
meet for the Master's use, and prepared unto
every good work"—2 Timothy 2:21.

Paul had spoken of the foundation of God standing sure (Timothy 2:19), of the Church as the
great house built upon that foundation of vessels,
not only of gold and silver, costly and lasting; but
also of wood and of earth, common and perisha-
ble. He distinguishes between those about whom
he spoke, those who gave themselves to striving
for words of praise, and those who truly sought to
depart from all iniquity. Paul gives us the four
steps of the path in which a man can become a
vessel unto honor in the great household of God.
These are: the cleansing from sin; being sanctified;
the suitability for the Master to use as He will; and
finally, the spirit of preparedness for every good
work. It is not enough that we desire or attempt to
do good works. As we need training and care to
prepare us for every work we are to do on earth,

we need to be prepared unto every *good* work that much more. It is this that constitutes the chief mark of vessels unto honor. *"If a man therefore purge himself from them."* A man must cleanse himself from that which characterizes the vessels of dishonor—the empty profession leading to ungodliness, against which Paul had warned. We insist that every dish and cup we use be clean. In God's house the vessels must be clean that much more. And every one who would be truly prepared unto every good work must first see that he cleanse himself from all that is sin. Christ Himself could not enter upon His saving work in heaven until He had accomplished the cleansing of our sins. How can we become partners in His work unless we first have the same cleansing. Before Isaiah could say, "Here am I; send me" (Isaiah 6:8), the fire of heaven had touched his lips, and he heard the voice, "thy sin (is) purged" (Isaiah 6:7). An intense desire to be cleansed from every sin lies at the root of fitness for true service.

"He shall be a vessel unto honour, sanctified." Cleansing is the negative side, the emptying out and removal of all that is impure. *Sanctified* is the positive side, the refilling and being possessed of the spirit of holiness, through whom the soul becomes God-possessed, and so partakes of His holiness. "Let us cleanse ourselves from all filthiness of the flesh and spirit"—this first, then, thus "perfecting holiness in the fear of God" (2 Corinthians 7:1). In the temple the vessels were not only to be clean, but holy, devoted to God's ser-

vice alone. He that would truly work for God must follow after holiness—"To the end that He may stablish your hearts unblameable in holiness before God" (1 Thessalonians 3:13), a holy habit of mind and disposition, yielded up to God and marked by a sense of His presence, fit for God's work. The cleansing from sin secures the filling with the Spirit.

"Meet for the Master's use." We are vessels for our Lord to use. In every work we do, it is to be Christ using us and working through us. The sense of being a servant, dependent on the Master's guidance, working under the Master's eye, instruments used by Him and His mighty power, lies at the root of effectual service. It maintains that unbroken dependence, that quiet faith, through which the Lord can do His work. It keeps up that blessed consciousness of the work being all His, which leads the worker to become more humble the more he is used. His one desire is—meet for the Master's use.

"Prepared unto every good work." Prepared. The word not only means equipment, fitness, but also the disposition, the cheerful readiness which keeps a man on the outlook, and makes him earnestly desire and joyfully avail himself of every opportunity of doing His Master's work. As he lives in touch with his Lord Jesus, and holds himself as a cleansed and sanctified vessel, ready for Him to use, and he sees that he was redeemed for good works, they become the one thing for which he lives and proves his fellowship with his Lord. He

is prepared unto every good work.

1. "Meet for the Master's use," that is the central thought. A personal relationship to Christ, an entire surrender to His disposal, a dependent waiting to be used by Him, a joyful confidence that He will use us—such is the secret of true work.

2. Let the beginning of your work be a giving yourself into the hands of the Master, as your living, loving Lord.

Chapter 20

Furnished Completely Unto Every Good Work

"Study to shew thyself approved unto God, a workman that needeth not to be ashamed, rightly dividing the word of truth"—2 Timothy 2:15.

"All scripture is given by inspiration of God, and is profitable for doctrine, for reproof, for correction, for instruction in righteousness: That the man of God may be perfect, thoroughly furnished unto all good works"—2 Timothy 3:16,17.

A workman that does not need to be ashamed is one who is not afraid to have the master come and inspect his work. In hearty devotion to it, in thoroughness and skill, he presents himself approved to him who employs him. God's workers are to present themselves approved to Him to have their work worthy and well-pleasing unto Him. They are to be as a workman that does not need to be ashamed. A workman is one who knows his work, who gives himself completely to it, who is known as a working man, who takes delight in doing his work well. Thus, every Christian minister, every Christian worker, is to be a workman who concentrates on inviting and expecting the Master's approval.

"Rightly dividing the word of truth." The Word is a seed, a fire, a hammer, a sword, bread, light. Workmen in any of these areas can be our example. In work for God, everything depends upon handling the Word correctly. Therefore, the one means of our being completely equipped to every good work is given in the scripture beginning this paragraph—personal subjection to the Word and the experience of its power. God's workers must know that Scripture is inspired of God, and has life-giving power in it. Inspiration is Spirit-breathed—as the life in a seed, God's Holy Spirit is in the Word. The Spirit in the Word and the Spirit in our heart is one. By the power of the Spirit within us we take the Spirit-filled Word. Thus, we become spiritual men. This Word is given for *teaching*—the revelation of the thoughts of God; for *reproof*—the discovery of our sins and mistakes; for *correction*—to remove what is defective and replace it by what is good; also for *instruction*—the communication of all the knowledge needed to walk before God righteously.

As one yields himself heartily to all this, and the true Spirit-filled Word gets mastery of his whole being, he becomes a man of God, furnished completely to every good work. He becomes a workman approved of God who does not need to be ashamed, rightly handling the Word of God. And so the man of God has the double mark—his own life completely molded and his work directed by applying the Word.

"That the man of God may be perfect, thoroughly furnished unto all good works." In the previous chapter we learned how the cleansing and sanctification of the personal life changes the worker into a vessel *meet for the Master's use, prepared unto every good work.* Here we learn the same lesson—it is the man of God who allows God's Word to do its work of reprimanding and correcting and instructing. Every worker for God must aim to be equipped for every good work.

A worker, aware of how defective his preparation is, might ask how this furnishing for every good work is to be attained. The analogy of an earthly workman, not needing to be ashamed, suggests the answer. The earthly worker would tell us that he owes his success, first of all, to devotion to his work. He gave it his close attention. He left other things to concentrate his efforts on mastering one thing. He made it a life-study to do his work perfectly. They who would do Christ's work as a second thing, not as the first, and who are not willing to sacrifice all for it, will never be fully equipped to every good work.

The second thing he will speak of will be patient training and exercise. Proficiency only comes through painstaking effort. You may feel as if you do not know how to work correctly. Have no fear. All learning begins with ignorance and mistakes. Be of good courage. He who has endowed human nature with the wonderful power that has filled the world with such skilled and cunning workmen, will give His children the grace they need to be His fellow-workers even more, will He not? Let the necessity that is laid upon you—the necessity that you should glorify God, that you should bless the world, that you should through work, advance and perfect your life and blessedness, urge you to give immediate and continual diligence to be a workman equipped unto every good work.

It is only in doing that we learn to do correctly. Begin working under Christ's training. He will perfect His work in you and make you fit for your work for Him.

1. The work God is doing, and seeking to have done in the world, is to win it back to Himself.

2. In this work every believer is expected to take part in this work.

3. God wants us to be skilled workmen, who give our whole heart to His work, and delight in it.

4. God does His work by working in us, inspiring and strengthening us to do His work.

5. What God asks is a heart and life devoted to Him in surrender and faith.

6. And God's work is all love, love is the power that works in us, inspiring our efforts and conquering its object.

Chapter 21

Zealous Of Good Works

"Who gave Himself for us, that He might redeem us from all iniquity, and purify unto Himself a peculiar people, zealous of good works"—Titus 2:14.

In these words we have two truths—what Christ has done to make us His own and what He expects of us. In the first part we have a rich and beautiful summary of Christ's work for us. He gave *Himself for us,* He redeemed us *from all iniquity,* He cleansed *us for Himself,* He took us for a people, *for His own possession.* And all with the one object—that we should be a people *zealous of good works.* The doctrinal half of this wonderful passage has had much attention given to it. Let us devote our attention to its practical part—we are to be a people zealous of good works. Christ expects us to be zealots for good works.

This cannot be said to be the feeling with which most Christians regard good works. What can be done to cultivate this disposition? One of the first things that awakens zeal in work is a great and urgent sense of need. A great need awakens strong desire, stirs the heart and the will, and rouses all the energies of our being. It was this sense of need that roused many to be zealous of the law. They hoped their works would save them. The Gospel has robbed this motive of its power. Has it entirely taken away the need of good works? No. Indeed, it has given that urgent need a higher place than before.

Christ needs our good works urgently. We are His servants, the members of His Body, without whom He cannot possibly carry on His work on earth. The work is so great (with millions of the unsaved) that not one worker can be spared. There are thousands of Christians today who feel that their own business is urgent and must be attended to, and have no conception of the urgency of Christ's work entrusted to them. The Church must wake up to teach each believer this.

The world needs our good works as urgently as Christ needs them. There are men, women, and children around you who need to be saved. To see men swept past us in a river stirs us to try and save them. Christ has placed His people in a perishing world with the expectation that they will give themselves, heart and soul, to carry on His work of love. Let us sound forth the blessed Gospel message: He gave Himself for us that He might redeem us for Himself, a people of His own, to serve Him and carry on His work—zealous of good works.

A second great element of zeal in work is delight in it. An apprentice or a student mostly begins his work under a sense of duty. As he learns to understand and enjoy it, he does it with pleasure and becomes zealous in its performance. The Church must train Christians to believe that when once we give our hearts to it, and seek for the training that makes us in some degree skilled workmen, there is no greater joy than that of sharing in Christ's work of mercy and charity. As physical and mental activity gives pleasure and calls for the devotion and zeal of thousands, the spiritual service of Christ can awaken our highest enthusiasm.

Then comes the highest motive, the personal one of attachment to Christ our Redeemer. "For the love of Christ constraineth us" (2 Corinthians 5:14). The love of Christ, to us, is the source and measure of our love to Him. Our love to Him becomes the power and the measure of our love to souls. This love, poured forth widely in our hearts by the Holy Spirit, becomes a zeal for Christ that shows itself as a zeal for good works. It becomes the link that unites the two parts of our text, the doctrinal and the practical, into one. Christ's love redeemed us, cleansed us, and made us a people of His own. When that love is believed in, known, and received into the heart, it makes the redeemed soul zealous in good works.

"Zealous of good works!" Let no believer look upon this grace as too high. It is divine, provided for and assured in the love of our Lord. Let us accept it as our calling. Let us be sure it is the very nature of the new life within us. Let us, in opposition to all that nature or feeling may say, in faith

claim it as an integral part of our redemption—
Christ Himself will make it true in us.

Chapter 22

Ready To Every Good Work

"Put them in mind. . .to be ready to every good work"—Titus 3:1.

"Put them in mind." The words suggest the need of believers to have the truths of their calling to good works set before them again and again. A healthy tree spontaneously bears its fruit. Even where the life of the believer is in perfect health, Scripture teaches us how its growth and fruitfulness can only come through teaching and the influence that exerts on mind and will and heart. For all who have charge of others the need of divine wisdom and faithfulness is great in order to teach and train all Christians. Let us consider some of the chief points of such training.

Teach them clearly what good works are. Lay the foundation in the will of God, as revealed in the law, and show them how integrity and righteousness and obedience are the groundwork of Christian character. Teach them how, in all the duties and relationships of daily life, true religion is to be carried out. Lead them on to the virtues which Jesus especially came to exhibit and teach—humility, meekness, gentleness, and love. Explain to them the meaning of a life of love, self-sacrifice, and charity—entirely dedicated to thinking of and caring for others. And then carry them on to what is the highest, the true life of good works—the winning of men to know and love God.

Teach them what an essential part of the Christian life good works are. They are not, as many think, a secondary element in the salvation which God gives. They are not merely to be done in token of our gratitudes, or as a proof of the sincerity of our faith, or as a preparation for heaven. They are all this, but they are a great deal more. They are the very object for which we have been redeemed. We have been created anew unto good works. They alone are the evidence that man has been restored to his original destiny of working with, through, and in God. God has no higher glory than His works, particularly His work of saving love. In becoming imitators of God and walking and working in love, even as Christ loved us and gave Himself for us, we have the very image and likeness of God restored in us. The works of a man not only reveal his life, they develop, exercise, strengthen, and perfect it. Good works are the very essence of the divine life in us.

Teach them, too, what a rich reward they bring. All labor has its market value. From the poor man who can scarcely earn a little money, to the man who has made his millions, the thought of the reward for labor has been one of the great incentives to undertake it. Christ appeals to this feeling when He says, "your reward shall be great" (Luke 6:35). Let Christians understand that there is no service where the reward is so rich as that of God. Work is bracing, work is strength, and cultivates the sense of mastery and conquest. Work awakens enthusiasm and calls out a man's noblest qualities. In a life of good works, the Christian becomes conscious of his divine ministry of dispensing the life and grace of God to others. They bring us into closer union with God. There is no higher fellowship with God than fellowship in His saving work of love. It brings us into sympathy with Him and His purposes. It fills us with His love. It secures His approval. And great is the reward, too, on those around us. When others are won to Christ, when the weary and the erring and the desponding are helped and made partakers of the grace and life in Christ Jesus for them, God's servants share in the very joy in which our blessed Lord found His reward.

And now the chief thing—*Teach them to believe that it is possible for each of us to abound in good works.* Nothing is so fatal to successful effort as discouragment or despondency. Nothing is more a frequent cause of neglect of good works than the fear that we do not have the power to perform them. Put them in mind of the power of the Holy Spirit dwelling in them. Show them that God's promise and provision of strength is always equal to what He demands. Show them

100

sufficient grace is always available for all the good works to which we are called. Strive to awaken in them a faith in "the power that worketh in us" (Ephesians 1:20) and in the fullness of that life which can flow out as rivers of living water. Train them to begin their service of love at once. Lead them to see how it is all God working in them and to offer themselves as empty vessels to be filled with His love and grace. And teach them that as they are faithful in a little, even in the midst of mistakes and shortcomings, the acting out of the life will strengthen the life itself, and work for God will become in full truth a second nature.

God grant that the teachers of the Church may be faithful to its commission in regard to all her members—"Put them in mind to be ready for every good work." Not only teach them, but train them. Show them the work there is to be done by them. See that they do it. Encourage and help them to do it hopefully. There is no part of the office of a pastor more important, more sacred, or fuller of richer blessing. Let the aim be nothing less than to lead every believer to live entirely devoted to the work of God in winning men to Him. What a change it would make in the Church and the world!

1. Get a firm hold of the great basic principle— Every believer, every member of Christ's body, has his place in the body solely for the welfare of the whole body.

2. Pastors have been given for the perfecting of the saints with the work of ministering, of serving

101

in love.

3. In ministers and members of the churches, Christ will work mightily if they will wait upon Him.

Chapter 23

Careful To Maintain Good Works

"I will that thou affirm constantly, that they which have believed in God might be careful to maintain good works. . . .And let ours also learn to maintain good works for necessary uses, that they be not unfruitful"—Titus 3:8,14.

In the first part of these passages, Paul charges Titus to state confidently the truths of the blessed Gospel to the end, with the express object that all who had believed *should be careful,* should make a study of it, *to maintain good works.* Faith and good works were to be inseparable. The diligence of every believer in good works was to be a main aim of a pastor's work. In the second passage he repeats the instruction, with the expression *let them learn.* As all work on earth has to be learned, so in the good works of the Christian life there is an equal need of thought and application and teachableness to learn how to do them correctly and abundantly.

There may be more than one reader of this book who has felt how little he has lived in accordance with all the teaching of God's Word, prepared, thoroughly equipped, ready unto, zealous of, good works. It appears so difficult to: get rid of old habits, to break through the conventionalities of society, and to know how to begin and really enter upon a life that can be full of good works to the glory of God. Let me try and give some suggestions that may be helpful. They may also aid those who have the training of Christian workers, in showing in what way the teaching and learning of good works may best succeed.

1. *A learner must begin by beginning to work at once.* There is no way of learning an art like swimming or music, a new language or a trade, but by practice. Let neither the fear that you cannot do it, nor the hope that something will happen that will make it easier for you, keep you back. Learn to do good works, the works of love, by beginning to do them. However insignificant they appear, do them. A kind word, a little help to someone in trouble, an act of loving attention to a stranger or a poor man, the sacrifice of a seat or a place to someone who longs for it—practice these things. All plants we cultivate are small at first. Cherish the consciousness that, for Jesus' sake, you are seeking to do what would please Him. It is only in doing you can learn to do.

2. *The learner must give his heart to the work and must take interest and pleasure in it.* Delight in work ensures success. Let the tens of thousands around you in the world who throw their whole soul into their daily business teach you how to

serve your blessed Master. Think sometimes of the honor and privilege of doing good works, of serving others in love. It is God's own work, to love and save and bless men. He works it in you and through you. It makes you share the spirit and likeness of Christ. It strengthens your Christian character. Without actions, intentions lower and condemn a man instead of raising him. You only really live as much as you act out. Think of the godlike blessedness of doing good, of communicating life, of making happy. Think of the exquisite joy of growing up into a life of charity and being the blessing of all you meet. Set your heart upon being a vessel fit for the Master's use, ready to do every good work.

3. *Be of good courage, and fear not*. The learner who says I cannot, will surely fail. There is a divine power working in you. Study and believe what God's Word says about it. Let the holy self-reliance of St. Paul, grounded on his reliance on Christ, be your example—"I can do all things through Christ which strengtheneth me" (Philippians 4:13). Study and take to heart the wonderful promises about the power of the Holy Spirit, the abundance of grace, Christ's strength made perfect in weakness, and see how all this can only be made true to you *in working*. Cultivate the noble consciousness that as you have been created to good works by God, He Himself will fit you for them. And believe, then, that just as natural as it is to any workman to delight and succeed in his profession, it can be natural to the new nature in you

to abound in every good work. Having this confidence, you never need to faint.

4. *Above all, cling to your Lord Jesus as your Teacher and Master.* He said: "Learn of Me; for I am meek and lowly in heart: and ye shall find rest unto your souls" (Matthew 11:29). Work as one who is a learner in His school, who is sure that none teaches like Him. Cling to Him, and let a sense of His presence and His power working in you make you meek and lowly, and yet bold and strong. He who came to do the Father's work on earth, and found it the path to the Father's glory will teach you what it is to work for God.

To sum up again, for the sake of any who want to learn how to work, or how to work better:

1. Yield yourself to Christ. Lay yourself on the altar and say you wish to give yourself completely for God's work.

2. Believe quietly that Christ accepts and takes charge of you for His work and will equip you for it.

3. Pray much that God would open to you the great truth of His own working in you. Nothing else can give true strength.

4. Seek to cultivate a spirit of humble, patient, trustful dependence upon God. Live in loving fellowship and obedience to Christ. You can count upon His strength being made perfect in your weakness.

Chapter 24

As His Fellow-Workers

"For we are labourers together with God: ye are God's husbandry, ye are God's building"—1 Corinthians 3:9.

"We then, as workers together with Him, beseech you also that ye receive not the grace of God in vain"—2 Corinthians 6:1.

We have listened to Paul's teaching on good works (chapters 9 and 22). Let us turn now to his personal experience and see if we can learn some of the secrets of effective service from him.

He speaks here of the Church as God's building, which as the Great Architect, He is building up into a holy temple and dwelling for Himself. Of his own work, Paul speaks as a master builder, to whom a part of the great building has been given his charge. He had laid a foundation in Corinth. To all who were working there he said: "For we are labourers together with God. . .Let every man take heed how he buildeth thereupon" (1 Corinthians 3:9,10). The word is applicable not only to Paul, but to all God's servants who take part in His work. And because every believer has been called to give his life to God's service and to win others to His knowledge, every Christian needs to have the Word brought to him and taken home—We are God's fellow-workers. How much it suggests in regard to our working for God!

As to the work we have to do—The eternal God is building for Himself a temple. Jesus Christ, God's Son, is the foundation. Believers are the living stones. The Holy Spirit is the mighty power of God through which believers are gathered out of the world, made fit for their place in the temple, and built up into it. As living stones, believers are at the same time the living workmen, whom God uses to carry out His work. They are equally God's workmanship and God's fellow-workers. The work God is doing He does through them. The work they have to do is the very work God is doing. God's own work, in which He delights, on which His heart is set, is saving men and building them into His temple. This is the one work on which the heart of everyone who would be a fellow-worker with God must be set. It is only as we know how great this work of God is—giving life to dead souls, imparting His own life to them, and living in them—that we will enter into the glory of our work. We will receive the very life of God and pass it on to men.

As to the strength for the work—Paul says of his work as a mere master builder, that it was "according to the grace of God which is given unto me" (1 Corinthians 3:10). For divine work nothing but divine power suffices. The power by which God works must work in us. That power is His Holy Spirit. Study the second chapter of 1 Corinthians and the third chapter of 2 Corinthians. You will see how absolute was Paul's acknowledgment of his own impotence, and his dependence on the teaching and power of the Holy Spirit. The truth is God's work can only be done by God's power in us. Our first need every day is to have the presence of God's Spirit renewed within us.

The power of the Holy Spirit is the power of love. God is love. All He works for the salvation of men is love. It is love alone that truly conquers and wins the heart. In all God's fellow-workers love is the power that reaches the hearts of men. Christ conquered and conquers still by the love of the cross. Let that mind be in you, which was in Christ Jesus—the spirit of a love that sacrifices itself to the death, of a humble, patient, gentle love—and you will be made fit to be God's fellow-worker.

As to the relationship we are to hold to God— In executing the plans of a great building, the master builder has but one care—to carry out to the minutest detail the thoughts of the architect who designed it. He acts in constant consultation with him, and is guided in all by his will. His instructions to those under him have all reference to the one thing—the embodiment, in visible shape, of what the master mind has conceived. The one great characteristic of fellow-workers with God ought to be that of absolute surrender to

109

His will, unceasing dependence on His teaching, and exact obedience to His wishes. God has revealed His plan in His Word. He has told us that His Spirit alone can enable us to enter into His plans, and fully master His purpose with the way he desires to have it carried out.

We must have clear insight into the divine glory of God's work of saving souls. We must see the utter insufficiency of our natural powers to do the work. We must know that He has made provision to strengthen and guide us in performance. We will then come to a greater understanding that a childlike teachableness (a continual looking upward and waiting on God) is to always be the chief mark of one who is His fellow-laborer.

Out of the sense of humility, helplessness, and nothingness there will grow a holy confidence and courage. We will know that our weakness need not hinder us, that Christ's strength is made perfect in weakness, that God Himself is working out His purpose through us. And of all the blessings of the Christian life, the most wonderful will be that we are allowed to be—God's fellow-workers!

1. God's fellow-worker! How easy to use the word, and even to apprehend some of the great truths it contains! How little we live in the power and the glory of what it actually involves!

2. Fellow-workers with God! Everything depends upon knowing, in His holiness and love, the God with whom we are associated as partners.

3. He who has chosen us, will fit us for His use that in and through us He might do His great work.

4. Let our posture be adoring worship, deep dependence, great waiting, and full obedience.

Chapter 25

According To The Working Of His Power

"Whom we preach, warning every man, and teaching every man in all wisdom; that we may present every man perfect in Christ Jesus: Whereunto I also labour, striving according to His working, which worketh in me mightily"—Colossians 1:28-29.

"The mystery of Christ. . . .Whereof I was made a minister, according to the gift of the grace of God given unto me by the effectual working of His power"—Ephesians 3:4,7.

In the words of Paul to the Philippians, which we have already considered in chapter nine, he called upon them and encouraged them to work because it was God who worked in them. This is one of the most momentous and comprehensive statements of the great truth that it is only by God's working in us that we can do true work. In our texts for this chapter, we have Paul's testimony about his own experience. His whole ministry was to be according to the grace which was given him according to the working of God's power. He says that His labor was a striving according to the power of Him who worked mightily in him.

We find here the same principle we found in our Lord—the Father doing the works in Him. Let every worker who reads this pause and say—"if the ever-blessed Son and Paul could only do their work according to the working of His power who worked mightily in them, how much more do I need this working of God in me!" This is one of deepest spiritual truths of God's Word. Let us look to the Holy Spirit within us to give it such a hold of our inmost life, that it may become the deepest inspiration of all our work. We can only do true work as we yield ourselves to God to work in us.

We know the ground on which this truth rests— "There is none good but one, that is, God" (Matthew 19:17). "There is none holy as the Lord" (1 Samuel 2:2). "Power belongeth unto God" (Psalm 62:11). All goodness and holiness and power are only to be found in God and where He gives them. He can only give them to man, not as something He parts with, but by His own actual presence and dwelling and working. God can only work in His people as He is allowed to have complete possession of their hearts and lives. As the will and life and love are yielded up in dependence and faith, and we wait on God as Christ waited on Him, God can work in us.

This is true of all our spiritual life, but especially of our work for God. The work of saving souls is God's own work. None but He can do it.

The gift of His Son is the proof of how great and precious He counts the work, and how His heart is set upon it. His love never for one moment ceases working for the salvation of men. And when He calls His children to be partners in His work, He shares with them the joy and the glory of the work of saving and blessing men. He promises to work His work through them, inspiring and energizing them by His power working in them. To the individual who can say with Paul: "I also labour, striving according to His working, which worketh in me mightily," his whole relationship to God becomes the counterpart and the continuation of Christ's, a blessed, unceasing, momentary, and most absolute dependence on the Father for every word He spoke and every work He did.

Christ is our pattern. Christ's life is our law and works in us. Paul lived his life of dependence on God as Christ did. Why should any of us hesitate to believe that the grace given to Paul of laboring and striving "according to the working of the power" will also be given to us. Let every worker learn to say—As the power that worked in Christ worked in Paul too, that power works no less in me." There is no possible way of doing God's work correctly but by God working it in us.

How I wish that I could take every worker who reads this by the hand, and say—"Come. Let us quiet our minds, and hush every thought in God's presence, as I whisper in your ears the wonderful secret: *God is working in you. All the work you have to do for Him, God will work in you."* Take

114

time and think it over. It is a deep spiritual truth which the mind cannot grasp nor the heart realize. Accept it as a divine truth from heaven. Believe that this word is a seed from which the very spiritual blessing of which it speaks can grow. And in the faith of the Holy Spirit's making it live within you, always consider: *God worketh in me.* All the work I have to work for Him, God will work in me.

The faith of this truth, and the desire to have it made true in you, will compel you to live very humbly and closely with God. You will see how work for God must be the most spiritual thing in a spiritual life. And you will again and again bow in holy stillness and acknowledge that God is working in you and will continue to work in you. Like Paul you can say: "I will work for Him according to the power which worketh in me mightily."

1. The gift of the grace of God (Ephesians 2:7, 3:7), the power that worketh in us (Ephesians 3:20), the strengthening with might by the Spirit (Ephesians 3:16)—the three expressions all contain the same thought of God's working all in us.

2. The Holy Spirit is the power of God. Seek to be filled with the Spirit, to have your whole life led by Him, and you will become fit for God's working mightily in you.

3. "Ye shall receive power, after that the Holy Ghost is come upon you" (Acts 1:8). Through the Spirit dwelling in us God can work in us mightily.

4. What holy fear, what humble watchfulness and dependence, what entire surrender and obedi-

ence becomes us if we believe in God's working in us.

Chapter 26

Laboring More Abundantly

"By the grace of God I am what I am: and His grace which was bestowed upon me was not in vain; but I laboured more abundantly than they all: yet not I, but the grace of God which was with me"—1 Corinthians 15:10.

"And He said unto me, My grace is sufficient for thee: for My strength is made perfect in weakness. . .for in nothing am I behind the very chiefest apostles, though I be nothing"—2 Corinthians 12:9,11.

In both of these passages, Paul speaks of how he had abounded in the work of the Lord. "In nothing was I behind the chiefest apostles." "I laboured more abundantly than they all." In both he tells how entirely it was God who worked in him and not himself. In the first passage he says: "Not I, but the grace of God which was with me." And then in the second, showing how this grace is Christ's strength working in us. While we are nothing, he tells us: "He said unto me: My grace is sufficient for thee: My power is made perfect in weakness."

May God give us "the Spirit of wisdom and revelation" (Ephesians 1:17) and the enlightened eyes of the heart (see Ephesians 1:18) to see this wonderful vision of a man who knew himself to be nothing. He was a man who gloried in his weakness so that the power of Christ would rest on him and work through him and who labored more abundantly than all. What this teaches us as workers for God!

God's work can only be done in God's strength—It is only by God's power, that is, by God Himself working in us, that we can do effective work. Throughout this book this truth has been frequently repeated. It is easy to accept it. It is far from easy to see its full meaning—to give it the mastery over our whole being, to live it out. This will need stillness of soul, meditation, strong faith, and fervent prayer. As it is God alone who can work in us, it is equally God *who alone can reveal Himself as the God who works in us.* Wait on Him, and the truth that ever appears to be beyond your reach will be opened up to you through the knowledge of who and what God is. When God reveals Himself as *"God who worketh all in all,"* you will learn to believe and work "according to the power of Him who worketh in thee mightily."

God's strength can only work in weakness—It is only when we truly say, *"Not I,"* that we can fully say, *"but the grace of God with me."* The man who said, *"In nothing am I behind the very chiefest of the apostles,"* first had to learn to say *"though I be nothing."* He could say: "I take pleasure in infirmities. . .for when I am weak, then am I strong" (2 Corinthians 12:10). This is the true relationship between the Creator and mankind, between the divine Father and His child, between God and His servant. Christian worker! Learn the lesson of your own weakness, as the indispensable condition of God's power working in you. Do believe that to take time and to realize in God's presence your weakness and nothingness is the sure way to be clothed with God's strength. Accept every experience by which God teaches you your weakness as His grace preparing you to receive His strength. Take pleasure in weaknesses!

God's strength comes in our fellowship with Christ and His service—Paul says: "Most gladly therefore will I rather glory in my infirmities, that *the power of Christ* may rest upon me" (2 Corinthians 12:9). "I take pleasure in infirmities. . .*for Christ's sake"* (2 Corinthians 12:10). And he tells how it was when he had besought *the Lord* that the messenger of Satan might depart from him, that He answered: "My grace is sufficient for thee." "Christ (is) the power of God and the wisdom of God" (1 Corinthians 1:24). We do not receive the wisdom to know or the power to do God's will as something that we can possess and use at discretion. It is in the personal attachment to Christ, in a life of continual communication with Him, that His power rests on us. It is in taking pleasure in weaknesses for Christ's sake that Christ's strength is known.

God's strength is given to faith, and the work that is done in faith—A living faith is needed to take pleasure in weakness, and in weakness to do our work, knowing that God is working in us. The highest exercise of a life of faith is to go on in the confidence of a hidden power working in us, without seeing or feeling anything. Faith alone can do God's work in saving souls. Faith alone can persevere in prayer and labor. Faith alone can continue to labor more abundantly despite unfavorable circumstances and appearances. Let us be strong in faith, giving glory to God. God will show Himself strong towards him whose heart is perfect with Him.

Be willing to yield yourself to the very utmost to God, that His power may rest upon you and work in you. *Do let God work through you.* Offer yourself to Him for His work as the one object of your life. Count upon His working in you to fit you for His service and to strengthen and bless you in it. Let the faith and love of your Lord Jesus, whose strength is going to be made perfect in your weakness, lead you to live even as He did, to do the Father's will and finish His work.

1. Let every minister seek the full personal experience of Christ's strength made perfect in His weakness. This alone will fit him to teach believers the secret of their strength.

2. Our Lord says: "My grace, My strength." It is as, in close personal fellowship and love, we abide in Christ, and have Christ abiding in us, that His grace and strength can work.

3. It is a heart completely given up to God, to His will and love, that will know His power working in our weakness.

Chapter 27

A Doer Who Works Will Be Blessed In Doing

"But be ye doers of the word, and not hearers only, deceiving your own selves"—James 1:22.

"But whoso looketh into the perfect law of liberty, and continueth therein he being not a forgetful hearer, but a doer of the work, this man shall be blessed in his deed"— James 1:25.

God created us not to contemplate but to act. He created us in His own likeness, and in Him there is no thought without simultaneous action. True action is born of contemplation. True contemplation, as a means to an end, always causes action. There would never have been a separation between knowing and doing if sin had not entered the world. In nothing is the power of sin more clearly seen than this, that even in the believer there is such a gap between intellect and conduct. It is possible to delight in hearing, to be diligent in increasing our knowledge of God's Word, to admire and approve the truth, even to be willing to do it, and yet to fail entirely in the actual performance. Thus, James warns us not to delude ourselves with being hearers and not doers. Thus, he pronounces the doer who works as blessed in his doing.

Blessed in doing. The words are a summary of the teaching of our Lord Jesus at the close of the Sermon on the Mount: "Not every one that saith unto Me, Lord, Lord, shall enter the kingdom of heaven; but he that doeth the will of My Father" (Matthew 7:21). "Therefore whosoever heareth these sayings of Mine, and doeth them, I will liken him unto a wise man" (Matthew 7:24). To the woman who spoke of the blessedness of her who was his mother: "Yea rather, blessed are they that hear the word of God, and keep it" (Luke 11:28). To the disciples in the last night: "If ye know these things, happy are ye if ye do them" (John 13:17). It is one of the greatest dangers in religion that we are content with reorganizing with pleasure and approval the meaning of a truth, yet do not immediately perform what it demands! It is only when conviction has been translated into conduct that we have proof that the truth is mastering us.

A doer of the work, this man shall be blessed in his deed. The doer is blessed. The doing is the victory that overcomes every obstacle. It brings out and confirms the very image of God, the Great Worker. It removes every barrier to the enjoyment of all the blessing God has prepared. We are ever inclined to seek our blessedness in what God gives in privilege and enjoyment. Christ placed it in what we do because it is only in doing that we really prove and possess the life God has bestowed. When one said, "Blessed is he that shall eat bread in the kingdom of God" (Luke 14:15), our Lord answered with the parable of the supper (see Luke 14). The doer is blessed. It is only in doing that the painter or musician, the man of science or commerce, the discoverer or the conqueror find their blessedness. So, and much more, is it only in keeping the commandments and in doing the will of God that the believer enters fully into the truth and blessedness of fellowship with God and deliverance from sin. Doing is the very essence of blessedness, the highest manifestation, and therefore the fullest enjoyment of the life of God.

A doer of the work, this man shall be blessed in his deed. This was the blessedness of Abraham, of whom we read: "Seest thou how faith wrought with his works, and by works was faith made perfect?" (James 2:22). He had no works without faith. There was faith working with them and in them all. And he had no faith without works. Through them his faith was exercised and strengthened and perfected. As his faith, so his blessedness was perfected in doing. It is in *doing* that the doer who works is blessed. The true insight into this will make us take every command, every truth and every opportunity to abound in good works as an integral part of the blessedness of the salvation Christ has brought us. Joy and work, work and joy, will become synonymous. We shall no longer be hearers but doers.

Let us put this truth into immediate practice. Let us live for others, to love and serve them. If you think you are not able to labor for souls, begin with the bodies. Only begin and go on, and abound. Believe that "It is more blessed to give than to receive" (Acts 20:35). Pray for and depend on the promised grace. Give yourself to a ministry of love. In the example of Christ and in the promise of God, you have the assurance. If you know these things, *happy are you if you do them.* Blessed is the doer!

Chapter 28

The Work Of Soul-Saving

"Brethren, if any of you do err from the truth, and one convert him; Let him know, that he which converteth the sinner from the error of his way shall save a soul from death, and shall hide a multitude of sins"—James 5:19-20.

We sometimes hesitate to speak of men being converted and saved by men. Scripture here twice uses the expression of one man converting another, and once of his saving him. Let us not hesitate to convert and save men, for it is God who works in us.

"Shall save a soul from death." Every workman studies the material in which he works—the carpenter the wood, the goldsmith the gold. Our "deeds. . .are wrought in God" (John 3:21). In our good works we deal with souls. Even when we can at first do no more than reach and help their bodies, our aim is the soul. For these Christ came to die. For these God has appointed us to watch and labor. Let us study the habits of these people. What care a hunter or a fisherman takes to know

the habits of the spoil he seeks. Let us remember that it needs divine wisdom and training and skill to become winners of souls. The only way to get that training and skill is to begin to work. Christ Himself will teach each one who waits on Him.

The Church with its ministers has a part to take in that training. The daily experience of ordinary life proves how often unexpected powers exist in a man. When a man becomes conscious and master of the power there is in himself, he is a new creature. The power and enjoyment of life is doubled. Every believer has hidden within himself the power of saving souls. The kingdom of heaven is within us as a seed. Everyone of the gifts and graces of the Spirit are also a hidden seed. The highest aim of the ministry is to awaken the consciousness of this hidden seed of power to save souls. A depressing sense of ignorance or impotence keeps many back. James writes: "Let him *know,* that he which converteth the sinner. . .shall save a soul from death." Every believer needs to be taught to know and use the wondrous blessed power with which he has been endowed. When God said to Abraham: "I will bless thee, and. . .shall all the nations of the earth be blessed" (Genesis 22:17,18), He called him to a faith not only in the blessing that would come to him from above, but in the power of blessing he would be in the world. It is a wonderful moment in the life of a child of God when he sees that the second blessing is as sure as the first.

"He shall save a soul." Our Lord bears the

name of Jesus, Savior. He is the embodiment of God's saving love. Saving souls is His own great work. As our faith in Him grows to know and receive all there is in Him, as He lives in us and dwells in our heart and disposition, saving souls will become the great work to which our lives will be given. We shall be the willing and intelligent instruments through whom He will do His mighty work.

"If any of you do err from the truth, and one convert him. . .he which converteth the sinner. . .shall save a soul." The words suggest personal work. We chiefly think of large gatherings to whom the Gospel is preached. The thought here is of one who has erred and is sought after. We increasingly do our work through associations and organizations. "If *one* convert him, *he* saveth a soul." It is the love and labor of some individual believer that has won the erring one back. It is this we need in the Church of Christ—every believer who truly follows Jesus Christ looking out for those who are erring from the way, loving them, and laboring to help them back. Not one of us may say (as in Genesis 4:9) "Am I my brother's keeper?" We are in the world only and solely as the members of Christ's Body that we may continue to carry out His saving work. As saving souls was and is His work, His joy, His glory, let it be ours. Let each give himself personally to watch over individuals and seek to save them one by one.

"Know that he which converteth the sinner. . .shall save a soul." "If ye *know* these

things, happy are ye if ye *do* them" (John 13:17). Let us translate these Scripture truths into action. Let us give these thoughts shape and substance in daily life. Let us prove their power over us and our faith in them, by *work*. Is there a Christian around us wandering from the way, needing loving help and willing to receive it? Are there some whom we could take by the hand and encourage to begin again? If we are truly at the disposal of Jesus Christ, He would use us to show others the right way.

If we feel afraid—let us believe that the love of God dwells within us, not only calling but enabling us to do the work. Let us yield ourselves to the Holy Spirit to fill our hearts with that love, and fit us for its service. Jesus, the Savior, lives to save. He dwells in us. He will do His saving work through us. *"Know that he which converteth the sinner. . .shall save a soul from death, and shall hide a multitude of sins."*

1. More love to souls, born out of fervent love to the Lord Jesus—this is our great need.

2. Let us pray to love in the faith. As we exercise the little we have, more will be given.

3. Lord! Open our eyes to see Thee doing Thy great work of saving men, and waiting to give Thy love and strength into the heart of every willing one. Make each one of Thy redeemed a soul-winner.

Chapter 29

Praying And Working

"If any man see his brother sin a sin which is not unto death, he shall ask, and He shall give him life for them that sin not unto death"—1 John 5:16.

"And let us consider one another to provoke unto love and to good works." These words in Hebrews 10:24 express what lies at the very root of a life of good works—the thoughtful loving care we have for each other, that not one may fall away. As it is in Galatians 6:1: "If a man be overtaken in a fault, ye which are spiritual, restore such an one in the spirit of meekness." Jude writes of Christians who were in danger of falling away: "Others save with fear pulling them out of the fire; hating even the garment spotted by the flesh" (verse 23). As Christ's doing good to men's bodies always aimed at winning their souls, all our ministry of love must be subordinated to that which is God's great purpose and longing—the salvation unto life eternal.

Praying and working must always go together in

this labor of love. At times prayer may reach those whom words cannot reach. At times prayer may chiefly be needed for ourselves, to obtain the wisdom and courage for the words. As a rule, praying and working must be inseparable—the praying to obtain from God what we need for the soul, the working to bring to it what God has given us. The words of John here are most suggestive as to the power of prayer in our labor of love. It leads us to think of prayer as a personal work with a very definite object and a certainty of answer.

Let prayer be a personal effort. *If any man see* his brother *he shall ask.* We are so accustomed to act through societies and associations that we are in danger of losing sight of the duty resting upon each of us to watch over those around him. Let every member of our bodies be ready to serve any other member. Every believer is to care for the fellow-believers who are within his reach, in his church, his house, or social circle. The sin of each is a loss and a hurt to the Body of Christ. Let your eyes be open to the sins of your brethren around you. Do not speak evil or judge or helplessly complain, but love and help and care and pray. Ask God to see your brother's sin in its sinfulness, its danger to himself, and its grief to Christ. However, God's compassion and deliverance are within reach. Shutting our eyes to the sin of our brethren around us is not true love. See it, and take it to God, and make it part of your work for God to pray for your brother and seek new life for him.

Let prayer be definite. If any man see *his brother*

sinning let him ask. We need prayer from a person for a person. Scripture and God's Spirit teach us to pray for all society, for the Church with which we are associated, for nations, and for special areas of work. This is most needful and blessed. But somehow more is needed—to make those with whom we come into contact subjects of our intercession. The larger supplications must have their place, but it is difficult to know when our prayers are answered regarding them. But nothing will bring God so near, will test and strengthen our faith, and make us know we are fellow-workers with God, as when we receive an answer to our prayers for individuals. It will quicken in us the new and blessed consciousness that we indeed have power with God. Let every worker seek to exercise this grace of taking up and praying for individual souls.

Count upon an answer. He shall ask, *and God will give him* (the one who prays) *life for them that sin.* The words follow on those in which John had spoken about the confidence we have of being heard, if we ask anything *according to His will.* There is often complaint made of not knowing God's will. But here there is no difficulty. "He will have all men to be saved" (1 Timothy 2:4). If we rest our faith on this will of God, we shall grow strong and grasp the promise: "He shall ask, and *God will give him life* for them that sin." The Holy Spirit will lead us, if we yield ourselves to be led by Him, to the souls God would have us take as our special care, and for which the grace of faith and persevering prayer will be given us. Let the wonderful promise; *God will give to him who asks life* for them who sin, stir us and encourage us to our priestly ministry of personal and definite intercession, as one of the most blessed among the good works in which we can serve God and man.

Praying and working are inseparable. Let all who work learn to pray well. Let all who pray learn to work well.

1. Let us pray confidently, and if need be perseveringly, for an individual who needs a close walk with God, and for the faith that we can overcome with Him.

2. In all our work for God, prayer must take a much larger place. If God is to work all, then our position is to be that of entire dependence waiting for Him to work in us. If it takes time to persevere and to receive in ourselves what God gives us for others, there needs to be a work and a labor in prayer.

3. Oh, that God would open our eyes to the glory of this work of saving souls, as the one thing God lives for, as the one thing He wants to work in us!

4. Let us pray for the love and power of God to come on us, for the blessed work of soul-winning.

Chapter 30

I Know Thy Works

"To the angel of the church in Ephesus. . .in Thyatira. . .in Sardis. . .in Philadelphia. . .in Laodicea write. . .I know thy works"—Revelations 2,3.

"I know thy works." These are the words of Him who walks in the midst of the seven golden candlesticks, and whose eyes are like a flame of fire. As He looks upon the churches, the first thing He sees and judges of is—the works. The works are the revelation of the life and character. If we are willing to bring our works into His holy presence, His words can teach us what our work ought to be.

To Ephesus He says: *"I know thy works,* and thy labour, and thy patience, and how thou canst not bear them which are evil. . .and hast borne, and hast patience, and for My name's sake hast laboured, and hast not fainted. Nevertheless I have somewhat against Thee, because thou hast *left thy first love. . .* repent, and *do the first works"* (Revelation 2:2-5). There was here much to praise—toil, patience, and zeal that had never grown

134

weary. But there was one thing lacking—the tenderness of the first love.

In His work for us, Christ gave us before and above everything His love, the personal tender affection of His Heart. In our work for Him, He asks us nothing less. There is a danger of work being carried on, and our even bearing much for Christ's sake, while the freshness of our love has passed away. And that is what Christ seeks. And that is what gives power. And nothing can compensate for it. Christ looks for the warm, loving heart, the personal affection which ever keeps Him the center of our love and joy.

Christian workers, see that all your work be the work of love, of tender personal devotion to Christ Jesus.

To Thyatira: "I know thy works, and charity, and service, and faith, and thy patience, and thy works; and the last to be more than the first. Notwithstanding I have a few things against thee, because thou sufferest that woman Jezebel, which calleth herself a prophetess, to teach and to seduce my servants to commit fornication" (Revelation 2:19-20). Here again the works are enumerated and praised. The last had even been more than the first. But then there is one failure—a false toleration of what led to impurity and idolatry. And then He adds of His judgments: "The churches shall know that I am He which searcheth the reins and hearts: and *I will give unto every one of you according to your works*" (Revelation 2:23).

Along with much of good works there may be

some one form of error or evil tolerated which endangers the whole church. In Ephesus there was zeal for orthodoxy, but a lack of love—here love and faith, but a lack of faithfulness against error. If good works are to please our Lord, if our whole lives must be in harmony with them, in entire separation from the world and its allurements, we must seek to be what He promised to make us, established in every good word and work. In His judgment our work will decide our value.

To Sardis: *"I know thy works,* that thou hast a name. . .and art dead. Be watchful, and *strengthen* the things which remain, that are ready to die: for I have *not found thy works perfect before God"* (Revelation 3:1,2).

There may be all the forms of godliness without the power and all the activities or religious organization without the life. There may be many works, and yet He may say: I have found no work of thine fulfilled before My God, none that can stand the test and be really acceptable to God as a spiritual sacrifice. In Ephesus it was works lacking in love, in Thyatira works lacking in purity, in Sardis works lacking in life.

To Philadelphia: *"I know thy works*. . .for thou hast a little strength, and hast kept My word, and hast not denied My name. . .Because thou hast kept the word of My patience, I also will keep thee"* (Revelation 3:8,10).

On earth Jesus had said: "He that *hath My commandments, and keepeth them,* he it is that loveth Me" (John 14:21). "The Father Himself loveth you, because ye have loved Me" (John 16:27). Philadelphia, the church for which there is no reproof, had this mark: its chief work, and the law of all its work, was *it kept Christ's Word,* not in an orthodox creed only, but in practical obedience. Let nothing less be the mark and spirit of all our work—a keeping of the Word of Christ. Full, loving conformity to His will will be rewarded.

To Laodicea: *"I know thy works,* that thou art neither cold nor hot. . . .thou sayest, I am rich, and increased with goods, and have need of nothing"* (Revelation 3:15,17). There is not a church without its works, its religious activities. And yet the two great marks of Laodicean religion, lukewarmness and self-complacence, may rob them of their worth. It is not only the need of a fresh and fervent love as Ephesus teaches us, but also the need of that poverty of spirit. The conscious weakness out of which the absolute dependence on Christ's strength for all our work will grow. It will no longer leave Christ standing at the door, but enthrone Him in the heart.

"I know thy works." He who tested the works of the seven churches still lives and watches over us. He is ready in His love to discover what is lacking, to give timely warning and help, and to teach us the path in which our works can be fulfilled before His God. Let us learn from Ephesus the lesson of fervent love to Christ, from Thyatira that of purity and separation from all evil, from Sardis that of the need of true life to give worth to work, from Philadelphia that of keeping His Word, and from Laodicea that of the poverty of spirit which possesses the Kingdom of heaven and gives Christ the throne of all! Workers! Let us live and work in Christ's presence. He will teach, correct and help us, and one day give the full reward of all our works because they were His own works in us.

Chapter 31

That God May Be Glorified

"If any man speak, let him speak as the oracles of God; if any man minister, let him do it as of the ability which God giveth: that God in all things may be glorified through Jesus Christ, to whom be praise and dominion for ever and ever. Amen"—1 Peter 4:11.

Work is not done for its own sake. Its value consists in the object it attains. The purpose of him who commands or performs the work gives it its real worth. And the clearer a man's insight into the purpose, the better equipped he will be to take charge of the higher parts of the work. In erecting a splendid building, the purpose of the day-laborer may simply be as a hireling to earn his wages. The trained stone-cutter has a higher object—he thinks of the beauty and perfection of the work he does. The master mason has a wider range of thought. His aim is that all the masonry shall be true and good. The contractor for the whole building has a higher aim—that the whole building shall perfectly correspond to the plan he has to carry out. The architect has a still higher purpose—that the great principles of art and beauty might find their full expression in material shape. With the owner we find the final end—the use to which the grand structure is to be put when he presents the building as a gift for the benefit of his townsmen. All who have worked on the building honestly have done so with some true purpose. The deeper the insight and the keener the interest in the ultimate design, the more important the share in the work, and the greater the joy in carrying it out.

Peter tells us what our aim ought to be in all Christian service—"that in all things God may be glorified through Jesus Christ." In the work of God, a work not to be done for wages but for love, the humblest laborer is admitted to share in God's plans, and to an insight into the great purpose which God is working out. That purpose is nothing less than this—that God may be glorified. This is the one purpose of God, the great worker in heaven, the source and master of all work, that the glory of His love and power and blessing may be shown. This is the one purpose of Christ, the great worker on earth in human nature, the example and leader of all our work. This is the great purpose of the Holy Spirit, the power that works in us, or, as Peter says here, "the ability which God giveth." As this becomes our deliberate, intelligent purpose, our work will rise to its true level, and lift us into living fellowship with God.

"That God in all things may be glorified." What

140

does this mean? The glory of God is this, that He alone is the Living One, who has life in Himself. Yet not for Himself alone, but because His life is love for men as much as for Himself. This is the glory of God, that He is the only and ever-flowing fountain of all life and goodness and happiness, and that His creatures can have all this only as He gives it and works it in them. His working all in all, this is His glory. And the only glory His creature, His child, can give Him is this—receiving all He is willing to give, yielding to Him to let Him work, and then acknowledging that He has done it. Thus God Himself shows forth His glory in us. In our willing surrender to Him and our joyful acknowledgment that He does all, we glorify Him. And so our life and work is glorified, as it has one purpose with all God's own work, "that God in all things may be glorified through Jesus Christ, to whom be praise and dominion for ever and ever."

See here the spirit that elevates and consecrates Christian service. According to Peter: "If any man minister (in ministering to the saints or the needy), let him do it as *of the ability which God giveth*." Let us cultivate a deep conviction that God's work, down into the details of daily life, can only be done in God's strength, ". . .by the power that worketh in us" (Ephesians 3:20). Let us believe firmly and unceasingly that the Holy Spirit does dwell in us as the power from on high for all work to be done for on high. Let us in our Christian work fear nothing so much as working in our own human will and strength, and so losing the one thing needful in our work, God working in us. Let us rejoice in the weakness that renders us so absolutely dependent upon such a God, and wait in prayer for His power to take full possession.

"Let him do it as of the ability which God giveth: *that God in all things may be glorified through Jesus Christ.*" The more you depend on God alone for your strength, the more will He be glorified. The more you seek to make God's purpose your purpose, the more will you be led to give way to His working and His strength and love. I pray, that every worker might see what a nobility it gives to work, what a new glory to life, what a new urgency and joy in laboring for souls, when the one purpose has mastered us—that in all things God may be glorified through Jesus Christ.

1. The glory of God as Creator was seen in His making man in His own image. The glory of God as Redeemer is seen in the work He carries on for saving men, and bringing them to Himself.

2. This glory is the glory of His holy love, casting sin out of the heart, and dwelling there.

3. The only glory we can bring to God is to yield ourselves to His redeeming love to take possession of us, to fill us with love to others, and so through us to show forth His glory.

4. Let this be the one end of our lives—to glorify God; in living to work for Him, "as of the ability which God giveth"; and winning souls to know and live for His glory.

5. Lord! Teach us to serve in the ability which God giveth, that God in all things may be glorified

through Jesus Christ, to whom be praise and dominion for ever and ever. Amen